CONQUEROR
of the CLOUDS

William F. Hallstead

CONQUEROR
of the CLOUDS

ELSEVIER/NELSON BOOKS
New York

No character in this book is intended to
represent any actual person; all the incidents of the
story are entirely fictional in nature.

Library of Congress Cataloging in Publication Data

Hallstead, William F
  Conqueror of the clouds.

    I. Title.
PZ4.H193Co [PS3558.A395]   813'.54   80–12383
ISBN 0–525–66681–8

Published in the United States by Elsevier/Nelson Books,
a division of Elsevier-Dutton Publishing Company, Inc.,
New York. Published simultaneously in Don Mills,
Ontario, by Nelson/Canada.

Printed in the U.S.A.   First Edition
10 9 8 7 6 5 4 3 2 1

1

"The brake," the Studebaker salesman screeched. "The brake! *The brake!*"

Ben Horner rammed down on the pedal. The auto skidded sideways and jittered to a stop. A cloud of Clark Street dust rolled over the open machine and sifted into Ben's hair and down the collar of his work shirt.

The skinny salesman flipped off his straw boater and mopped his forehead with a blue bandanna. "That boy ran right in front of us! Did we hit him?" He jutted his head above the windscreen to squint into the settling dust.

"Of course we didn't hit him," Ben snorted as Eddie Driscoll trotted to the Studebaker's side.

"I've been all over Clarkston looking for you, Ben! Your uncle's going to skin you this time for sure." The slim blond boy stared. "What in tarnation are you doing behind the wheel of that thing?"

"What's it look like, Dris? I'm driving it."

The salesman slapped his straw hat back on his head. "You ought to watch where you're running, boy," he snapped at Dris. Then he grabbed Ben's arm. "What about our business deal?"

"What business deal?" Dris asked.

Ben swung down from the Studebaker. "Let's go, Dris."

"Hey, come back here!" the salesman yipped. He hopped over to the driver's seat, clashed the gears, and swung the auto around to roar up Clark Street after them.

"He's plenty burned up," Dris said as they broke into a trot. "What did you tell him?"

"Only that Uncle Alex was thinking of going into the garage business." Ben grinned.

"Your uncle working on gas buggies? You know he hates the things! What made you come up with a story like that?"

"I got to drive the auto, didn't I?" Ben's words were drowned in the approaching howl of the Studebaker. "He's gaining on us! Let's cut through between the feed store and Hanneker's."

The two boys veered off the dirt street and dashed through the narrow passage between the two stores. Behind them, the auto stopped, backfired, and the salesman stood up, shaking his fist.

"He'll find out where your uncle's blacksmith shop is and come over there for you, Ben," Dris panted as they slowed to a fast walk on Sycamore Street.

"No, he won't. He knows that I took him. That'll finish it. A fellow doesn't like to have people know he's been suckered."

Dris, a year younger than Ben, two inches shorter, and twenty pounds lighter, scowled. "It doesn't bother you a bit to pull that kind of trick, does it?"

"You got to take what you can when you can. Nobody looks out for you better than yourself."

They turned into Wabash Road, and Alex Horner's smithy came into view down the elm-shaded block. The storefronts thinned out here, and weedy vacant spaces appeared more frequently. This wasn't the best part of Clarkston. Farmers brought their horses and wagons here for work at Horner's or at Cable's Wagonry across the road. A few frame houses—the one next door to the smithy was Alex Horner's—edged the unpaved width of Wabash Road. Beyond, the road became a rutted country lane. It ran arrow straight through the flat Indiana fields, ending in the picnic grounds along the east bank of the sluggish Wabash River.

Ben had left one problem behind only to face another. His uncle stood, huge hands on his hips, in the wide entrance to the blacksmith shop. He was a giant of a man, with slicked-down black hair neatly parted in the middle, thick moustache waxed to points, arms like the giant sausages that hung in Fogleman's Market on Clark Street, and a neck like a prize fighter's. His face was crimson with anger.

"Why do you do this to me, boy? I've got two horses here to shoe, and you're nowhere to be seen. And if that ain't bad enough, I got to send Dris after you, and so he's no help here either. Where in thunder were you?"

Ben shrugged. What good would it do to lie? "Learning to drive an auto."

"Learning to drive an auto! If that don't beat all! I agreed with your pop to teach you a useful trade, and you're off playing with some rich man's toy. Get on in here and pump them bellows, Dris. Ben, you can swing a hammer well as anybody, and you know how Old Man Dowd wants his mare shod. Get at it, now, and stick at it. No more malarkey with autos!" He forced the word through a sour expression. "Damn useless things," he muttered, "stinking of gasoline and oil. Likely to blow up right under you." He grabbed a pair of tongs, yanked a glowing horseshoe from the charcoal fire, and gave it a savage slam with his hammer.

Ben eyed the chestnut mare and old Dexter, his uncle's road horse, tethered in stalls on the far side of the shop. There were worse smells in here than gasoline and oil, he thought. The sharp tang of the draft-forced charcoal fire, the scalded smell of hot metal, and the sweat of horses, mingled with his uncle's and his own. He hated it.

His hammer struck sparks from a shoe for Old Man Dowd's mare. He hated it more now than he had six months ago, when his father had sent him here from upstate. Ben had almost decided to keep on going, hooking rides on freight cars, but his father had spent almost his last dollar on Ben's train fare to Clarkston. Ben figured he owed his dad a few months here for that. But not much more. Not much more at all.

"Bring the mare over here, Dris," Alex Horner shouted. "Ben, put on that apron and pull the nails on her."

Ben stripped off his shirt and strapped on the leather apron. The heat in the shop was like a thick blanket.

"Now at least you look like a blacksmith," Uncle Alex grunted. "Let's see if you've got the muscle."

Ben yanked the mare's left hind foot off the hard-packed floor and straddled the ankle.

"Easy, boy. That's a living thing you're working with, not one of your smelly gas buggies."

"Horses aren't exactly perfume," Ben muttered.

"That's because you've got no nose for them. There's nothing in the world like the smell of good horses on a winter morning or after a summer buggy ride. You're still a city boy, Ben. I promised Evan I'd teach you everything I know about smithing, but you sure fight me every way you can. All right, now get that new shoe in place. I know you don't like any of this, but at least try to find some pride in doing it right."

He stood back and watched his nephew work. The boy was strong as a horse himself, a big strapping copy of brother Evan Horner in the days before Evan had married. Ben was close to six feet of solid muscle, with a strong jaw, a good straight nose, and clear gray eyes. But the eyes bothered Alex Horner. They had a hard look deep in them sometimes—too many times. Like now, when Ben had shown up after ducking out for most of the day. Alex didn't like that look.

In the late afternoon, they were finished. Old Man Dowd came by for the mare. Dris, with the coins he'd earned for the day's work jingling in his overalls, walked off toward his folks' farm a mile up Wabash Road. Uncle Alex lifted the loop of his apron over his head and shoved his arms into the checkered red shirt he took off a nail. "We'll call it a day, Ben." His anger had died through the work of the afternoon. "You're a hard driver, once you buckle down to it. No mistaking that. If only you'd take to the work more."

"I'll never take to this," Ben growled. "You're standing here getting old while the whole world moves right past you. It's 1912, but what you're doing belongs back in 1890."

"Just the same, it's a living. Come into the house. We'll eat."

Alex Horner was a limited but surprisingly good cook. "Man's as good at the stove as a woman," he'd told Ben.

"Them European mucky-muck chefs are all men; not a woman among them. I've always been good at taking care of myself. Maybe that's why I've never found a woman I could put up with for long. They want you to need them, and I don't. Needing them brings out the woman in them. They can't abide a man who's able to take care of himself. That's why I never got married, I suppose."

Tonight, though, Uncle Alex wasn't so talkative. He shoveled in his sausage and scrambled eggs, washed them down with scalding coffee, and then leaned forward with his elbows on the table.

They sat in the large kitchen. It was obvious that no woman's hand had ever worked in here. The window over the sink had a shade but no curtains. Flour, sugar, and salt were lined up on the counter in their store packaging. No bowl of flowers had ever decorated the table. But the kitchen was clean, freshly painted, and smelled pleasantly of fried food.

"You ever miss your mother?" he asked abruptly.

"No."

"I don't mean like a little boy might. I mean there's no woman here, and while that suits me, you're still—"

"I'm eighteen, Uncle Alex. All grown up. My mother has no use for me and I don't need her."

The blacksmith rubbed his chin. "You're pretty hard on her, Ben."

"She left me, she left my father. She found somebody else."

"She did stay until you were old enough to handle yourself. Give her that much."

Ben's eyes held a glint of anger. "If she could stay with my father for twenty years, I think she could have stayed still longer."

"Evan isn't the easiest man to get along with, meaning

no disrespect to my own brother. He's as headstrong as you, ambitious as you. Just as unthinking of others, too."

Ben's face flared crimson. "If you think I'm going to sit here and listen to you—"

"I think you ought to. I know I'm no father to you. More like a boss, I guess. But in the short time I've got to know you, I've come to think a lot of you, Ben. Somebody's got to set things straight for you, and it looks like Brother Evan didn't quite do that."

"He set me straight, all right. My mother was a no-good tramp."

"Now hold on there. You don't take enough trouble to understand people to be able to accuse your mother of anything like that!"

"I understand enough."

"No, you don't, either. You don't understand that your pop was quite a hand with the ladies before—and after— he was married. Again, I don't mean disrespect. That's just the way he's made. Your mother spent many a time wondering where he was and who he was with."

"He was on the road for the Pittsburgh Crockery Company."

"That's right, but that job made things mighty handy for him. And it made things mighty tough for your mother, sitting at home taking care of you, with no life of her own."

"That was her life," Ben said. "That's what women are supposed to do."

"Shows how much you understand them."

"You're not even married," Ben shot back. "What makes you such an expert?"

"Just because I'm not married don't mean I don't get to know some women, Ben. Know them better and more of them than most married men. One thing I know is that a woman's got her own life to live and her own needs to be filled if she's going to be happy. Your mother saw nothing ahead of her but loneliness. When that fellow from Atlanta showed up and they got to know one another . . . Well, that's the truth of it, Ben. It wasn't your mother was a bad woman. And I don't mean to say that your pop was a mean man. They were just two people who had to go their own ways, and that left you in the middle."

"In the blacksmith business."

"Why not in the blacksmith business? It's honest, hard work. You don't yet see the joy in beating a piece of hard iron into the shape you want it. You don't yet see the beauty in a white-hot forge fire or in the sound of a hammer ringing on the anvil. But stick at it, Ben, and you will."

Ben pushed back his chair and stood up. "No, I never will. Not ever. I'm not going to stay around here long enough for that."

2

The rattle and roar jolted Ben awake. He scrambled out of bed, tripped over the twisted sheet, and stumbled to the window. Automobiles had passed the house before, but this one sounded different.

He stuck his head out to peer up and down Wabash Road. Nothing. Not even settling dust. Odd . . . It couldn't have taken him ten seconds to get to the window.

He looked at the dollar New Haven clock on the dresser. Not yet six. He had a few minutes before Uncle Alex would expect him to be out in the smithy stoking the fire before breakfast. He lay back on the bed and linked his fingers behind his head. After last night, he had to admit to himself that he understood Alex Horner better— understood him but still didn't agree with him. Nailing shoes on plow horses and fixing the mistreated iron parts Sam Cable brought across the street from his wagon shop was all right for an old man without ambition. But the idea of spending the rest of his life in a stiff leather apron, sweltering in front of a forge fire, made Ben shudder.

His father had sent him here because it seemed to Evan Horner that there was no other choice.

"You can't stay with me, Ben," he had said in that soft voice so different from his brother's barrel-chested boom. "I'm on the road near all the time. I'm going to rent out this house so's I won't have to sell so hard for dear old Pittsburgh Crockery. Time's come for you to learn a trade, make your own way, now your mother's left us to fend for ourselves."

Ben had wondered why his father had taken his mother's departure so calmly. He'd seemed more depressed than angry. But if what Uncle Alex had told him last night was true, Ben's bitterness toward his mother was a bit askew. Sure, she had been the one who had stormed out of their little clapboard home in Indianapolis, but apparently his father had been far from blameless. Ben had loved them both, yet when trouble came between them, they had both deserted him. Ellen Horner had slammed the door behind her in a screaming tantrum. His father had put him on the train to Clarkston with a sad smile and a handshake, but he was turning his back on Ben, too.

Ben had learned plenty. If this was how life shaped up, he could live it as hard as anyone. And he was discovering that to look out for yourself without worrying about

16

anyone else worked wonders. That's how he'd gotten that free auto-driving lesson yesterday. That was how he would get a lot of things from now on.

To blazes with both his parents. To blazes with everybody! He was on his own now. There was nothing Alex Horner could do to keep him here once he made up his mind to go.

The alarm clock jangled. He reached out to slap it silent. The day had begun.

Dris ran into the smithy a full half hour early, his cornsilk hair flying. "Did you see it, Ben? Did you see it? It went right over my house!"

Ben quenched a hot shoe in the water tub with a whoosh of steam. "*Over* your house?"

"Dris," Alex Horner called across the barnlike shop, "you're early. Can't afford to pay you extra, but start now and I'll let you off early."

"It was an aeroplane!" Dris jabbered, grabbing Ben's arm. "A big white aeroplane. I think it came down near the river. I wanted to go look for it, but Ma and Pa wouldn't let me." He stole a look at Alex.

Ben slammed the horseshoe with his hammer. An aeroplane! He'd never seen one. "He's going into town to get a haircut," he said under his breath. "We'll have an easy morning. Maybe we could . . ."

Dris's eyes sparkled. "It was big, real big, with the driver sitting right up in front. And was it noisy!"

Realization struck Ben. "I heard it! About six o'clock. It came right over the house. No wonder I didn't see anything on the road. It must have come down close, it was so low when it went over."

"Boys!" shouted Alex Horner. "Stop moving your

17

mouths and start moving your legs and arms. There's plenty of work to be done."

With Dris pumping the forge bellows and toting charcoal, Ben custom-fashioned the whole set of shoes for Doc Miller's horse before his uncle finally laid down his own tools and lifted the apron strap over his head.

"I'm going on in, boys. No need to hitch up old Dexter. I'll walk. You're the boss while I'm gone, Ben. When you finish those, you and Dris clean out the back of the shop. Needs it bad. Put the trash out front in the bin. If I see Doc Miller in town, I'll tell him his roan's shoes are ready."

The big blacksmith took his checkered work shirt off the nail by the door, pulled it on, and walked down the ramp to the roadway. As he disappeared around the end of the building, a clatter rose along Wabash Road. Dris blanched.

"You're in for it, Ben! Sounds like that Studebaker salesman."

Ben laid down his hammer and cocked his head. "Doesn't sound like the same engine to me." He walked to the wide doorway and peered around it. "It's not. It's a tin lizzie."

A few yards down Wabash, a red-haired man was handing some sort of poster to Uncle Alex. The blacksmith glanced at it, then tried to hand it back. But the Ford's driver threw his auto in gear and bounced past. "Tack it up somewhere," he shouted. "We need all the good word we can get." Then the Model T was swallowed in dust as it jackrabbited toward the river.

Uncle Alex gazed after the auto, shrugged, ripped the poster in half, and tossed it in the bin at the edge of the road.

The boys waited long minutes for him to turn into Sycamore and walk safely out of sight. Then they raced to the trash bin. Ben grabbed the pieces and held them up together.

DARING AERONAUT
FOSTER PEPPERIDGE

in a

FLYING EXHIBITION
OF SUPERB SKILL
!!!!!!!!

ADMISSION FREE!!!

RIDE WITH THE
CONQUEROR OF THE CLOUDS

ONLY $5

!!!

Printed on pasteboard, the circus-style red type was splashed below a drawing of an aeroplane against a puffy cloud. Lettered by hand in the space at the bottom of the poster were the electrifying words: TODAY ONLY. NOON, NEAR PICNIC GROUNDS.

Ben stared at the poster. "I'm going," he announced. "Come with me if you want."

Dris took a fast look up Wabash where Sycamore crossed it. Ben knew his nerve was fading now that he was faced with actually going. Dris was like that. "My ma and pa'd skin me alive if your Uncle Alex was to find out that we—"

"Can't wait all day, Dris. Either you're coming or you aren't." He started down the road, Dris following uncertainly. The younger boy poked a thumb back at the smithy.

"Shouldn't we at least close the door?"

"We'll only be gone a short while. It's not much more'n a mile or so to the river. Here, hang my apron up." He struck off along the dirt road.

"Wait for me, Ben!"

"You can catch up." Though he was seventeen, Dris was a real tagalong, Ben thought. He worried about useless details—what his ma and pa would think, what Alex Horner would think, what anybody would think. You didn't get anywhere always wondering what everybody else thought of you.

The hard-packed road had dwindled into ruts along a newly planted cornfield when Dris panted up behind him.

"I banked the fire, Ben. You're a fast walker. I thought I'd never catch up."

"I didn't tell you to bank the fire."

"Thought I should. It'll be all right, now, till we get back. How long do you think we'll be?"

"I don't know, Dris. Quit worrying so much."

They trotted a full mile through the flat fields that were sprouting rows of spring corn and delicate shoots of new barley and wheat. Hedgerows bright with new leaves of sycamores and maples edged the broad open areas. The worn ruts became a lane, and the sun rose higher.

Dris wiped the sweat out of his eyes. "Ben, your uncle will—"

"Listen!"

Beyond the row of trees ahead of them, they heard the raggedy sawing of an engine. They stared at each other, then raced for the next hedgerow. Past it was the last field before the river, once a pasture, now a parking place for the buggies and autos that picnickers drove here on Sundays. It wasn't wide, but it was long and fairly smooth.

The tin lizzie was parked beneath a stand of maples. A hundred feet past it gleamed the white wings of an aeroplane, a big aeroplane, larger than Ben had imagined it would be. Its top wing was higher than his head, the double-decked main planes spanning perhaps forty feet.

Here was a mechanical miracle, right in front of him!

Then Ben scowled. As they walked closer, he realized that the machine's varnish was dull with age, and the wire rigging that bound the wings and their eighteen struts in a rigid box kite looked less taut than Ben imagined it should. The spars supporting the fragile tail plane and rudder showed crude field repairs. The dual skids projecting forward of the wings had been battered by rough landings, and the wheels mounted on either side of each skid wore patches. The fabric had long ago lost its true whiteness. It was yellowed and sagged stiffly between the ribs.

But altogether . . . Taken altogether, this was a flying machine! Ben could taste his excitement.

The rattling engine quit, and the twin wooden propellers behind the wings clanked to silence. A rasp of a voice proclaimed, "It's the fritterin' carburetor again, Murf. Won't feed. Just won't feed."

The owner of the rasp came up from behind the engine, which was bolted on the lower wing next to the side-by-side wooden seats. His hair stuck up in a graying cockscomb, and his reddish nose hooked like a small, sharp beak. A cockatoo, Ben thought.

"Yep, the fritterin' carburetor, Murf. Ain't worth the powder blown to pot." He walked around the wings wiping his hands on a rag. The man wore faded whipcord riding breeches and scuffed cavalry boots.

Ben nudged Dris. "That's got to be Pepperidge!"

They stared at the very first flyer they had ever set eyes on. Suddenly it didn't matter that he was nearly a foot shorter than either of them, wore a sweaty oil-stained shirt frayed at the elbows, and was stubbly-chinned and red-eyed. He lived in the clouds and the wind. The goggles hanging around his Adam's apple said so. He was part magician, part hero, part miracle. A flyer!

"Engine sucked in the chaff, Murf. Choked on it."

He seemed to be talking to the red-haired tin-lizzie driver in the once-white suit of coveralls. But the mechanic was bending over his tool kit, and the flyer looked mostly at the sky as he spoke. "Just choked up on it and won't feed."

Murf straightened up, a living scarecrow in those floppy coveralls. He shifted a plug of chewing tobacco into his left cheek, spat to one side, and fumbled in a pocket. "Think I got me a toothpick here. Let me at that thing."

Back beyond the hedgerow, Ben heard the sound of approaching autos. Murf heard it too.

"They're coming early, Fos," the mechanic said. "Told you this'd be a good burg. And you didn't want to come at all."

Pepperidge grunted. "These towns'll fool you. Just 'cause they're coming don't mean they'll buy rides. Most of these rubes come to gawk."

The line of autos began to jounce into the old pasture. Soon the aeroplane and the flyer would be surrounded by a crowd, Ben realized.

"What is it?" he asked quickly. "A Wright?"

Pepperidge's washed-out gray eyes focused somewhere over Ben's head, as if he were trying to locate an unattached voice. "Yeah." He was surprised that this hick kid had even heard of the word. "You know something about aeroplanes?"

"Read about them." There seemed no need for Ben to admit that the Wright was the only kind of aeroplane he could remember.

Pepperidge showed yellow teeth in a trace of a smile. "That so?" Ben caught a whiff of whiskey on his breath. "That so?"

"Fos!" Murf's voice twanged from behind the engine.

"Let's get things started. The crowd's building up. No time for jawing."

The rumpled pilot jammed the rag in the hip pocket of his breeches, picked his way through the forward skid's rigging, and planted his bony rump on the left-hand plywood seat. He joggled the levers and toggles, then reached across the empty seat and fiddled with the engine. "Contact!"

Murf wrapped his fingers around one of the two paddle-bladed pusher propellers behind the wings and gave it a tug. The engine hacked a gobbet of smoke. The propellers, connected to the engine by lengths of bicycle chain, whistled through two revolutions and froze.

Pepperidge pulled a cigar stump from a shirt pocket and jammed it between his teeth. "She's learning who's boss! Again, Murf."

The mechanic yanked, then leaped backward as the engine caught. The explosions blended into a steady rip. Pepperidge lifted his goggles into place and yelled, "All right, let's have the first passenger!"

As more and more autos and buggies had arrived, the crowd had grown. But no one moved forward.

"Come on, blang it! Ain't got all day. What's the matter with you folks?"

"Nothing the matter with me," a skinny man near Ben muttered. "And I want to keep it that way, not smashed to smithereens in that fool rig."

"Amen, brother," said a tall parsonlike man, folding his arms. "If God meant us to fly, he would have given us feathers."

Ben studied the crowd. There wasn't a lick of daring in any of them. And soon the chaff the propellers kicked up would choke the carburetor all over again.

23

The raggedy song of the engine overpowered Ben's hesitation. "Did you ever sell anything?" he said to Dris.

"Sell? No, never."

"Well, start!" He ran toward the trembling aeroplane. "Tell them they haven't got the guts or something." He scrambled through the bracing wires and Pepperidge bent down with a scowl.

"You got five bucks? No? Then get out of here, kid. This is business, blang it!" The flyer talked right in Ben's face, his whiskey breath overriding the smell of burning oil.

"It's no business at all," Ben shouted back. He was gripped by an excitement that gave him quick confidence. "You're going to spend all day running that engine and choking on chaff. They haven't got any faith in this thing. Take me up and they'll be shamed into it."

"You? For free? No money in that."

"We'll sell your rides," Ben shouted back. "Blang it!"

A grin spread around the dead cigar. "You got spunk, kid. Could use more of it around here, I'll tell you. Get up here!"

Ben boosted himself into the passenger seat. The wood vibrated against his rear, and the whole machine shook like a collapsing bridge. But it was unbelievably glorious up here on the wing! He looked out at the circling faces, cocked his head back and let a grin plaster itself across his face. At the edge of the crowd, Dris's jaw dropped. Ben made furious wallet-opening motions at him.

"Feet on that bar there, but don't do no pushing," Pepperidge ordered. "And keep your hands off the levers alongside the seat." The big aeroplane began to trundle down the pasture, pulling clear of the spectators. Murf ran alongside, head tilted toward them, making a last check of the engine's sound.

The roostery little pilot jammed his right foot forward

and Murf grabbed the lower wing. They bumped around a half circle to head into the wind.

The engine's blapping rose to a roar. The flying machine began to roll, then the bumps and jolts grew hard enough to propel Ben's hand to the only strut close enough to grab.

The wings flexed with each shock. The Wright was an old barnyard bird trying to get up enough speed for just one more flight. The hedgerows jittered past on both sides.

Then came the miracle. The ground, unrolling beneath Ben's feet like a moth-eaten carpet, fell away. The bouncing became as smooth as heavy cream. The engine's howl seemed to flatten into an efficient burble. A wall of warm wind pressed him into the seat, a magic throne from which he watched the pasture shrink beneath him. The Wabash River glittered beyond the falling trees. In the distance, Clarkston was a little cluster of dollhouses surrounded by the Indiana flatlands, which stretched to the horizon.

A miracle! He had done what only birds and a few incredible men had been able to do: He had sprung free of earth and touched the sky. The realization swept through him in a rush that left him gasping. He looked down the length of the wings. The aging fabric was taut now, riding on the cushion of air that whipped his hair, blasted tears from his squinting eyes, tugged at his cheeks. These thin planes of fragile wooden strips and simple cloth didn't seem capable of holding two people and a heavy engine in the air, but their lift was a solid force that changed invisible air into fluid support.

The old Wright swung around and Ben rode with the turn, not leaning away from the ground but staying upright in the seat. He had become part of the aeroplane, united with the machine in its every dip and bank. He saw the sideways glance of the flyer change from curiosity to approval. The turns grew steeper, as if Pepperidge were testing him. The force of each maneuver was a new sensation, and Ben saw the flyer smile to himself.

Then the engine's song faded to a grumble, and they sank toward the ground. The trees grew under Ben's feet, the pasture's boundary brush flashed beneath them, the ground once again seized the aeroplane in its jouncing grip.

It was over, but it would never really be over. Ben jumped to the grass on legs that threatened to race him forward to shout out the wonder of the flight. He tried for the careless gait of Pepperidge himself. He felt closer to the feisty Conqueror of the Clouds than to these earthlings who were afraid to step higher than a running board. He had been closer to the clouds than any of them. He was different now. He had flown.

"Sell some fritterin' rides!" the flyer's shout jabbed over the engine clatter. Ben nodded. Whatever Pepperidge said, he would do. However Pepperidge said it, he would do it. Pepperidge had shown him the sky.

"How is it?" Dris asked breathlessly, and Ben knew he could never properly describe what had taken place. You had to feel it, not be told about it. Telling was hopeless. "Swell!" he blurted. Swell? Lord! "How many rides have you sold?"

Dris grinned. "Two, if you can believe it! That old man and the boy. I have the money."

"Let's get the old man out there first. Nobody's going to let an old man show him up."

They escorted the grinning farmer to the aeroplane, one of them on either side because they were afraid he might bolt at the last minute, and they boosted him into the passenger seat. Dris offered Pepperidge the five one-dollar bills. "Hold on to it," Pepperidge shouted. "I trust you. Keep 'em coming!"

The biplane waddled to the head of the field, swung around and rattled past them, feeling for lift. In minutes, Pepperidge was back, drifting over the bushes and judging his landing roll to stop precisely in front of the onlookers. Ben and Dris got the freckled boy aboard next and brought forward a tough-looking fellow who had pressed his five dollars into Dris's hand as they'd waited for the old man to return. Ben realized there was some celebrity value in being the next to go, and he made the new buyer stand a good fifteen feet out from the crowd. The trick worked. Soon Dris led out another youthful man. Then, wonder of wonders, a girl of about twenty pulled her beau along with her, and they had sold six rides.

With one stop for refueling from cans aboard the Model T, the old flying machine hauled eleven paying passengers before the crowd wearied of what had become the machinelike precision of it all and evaporated back toward Clarkston, leaving a dusty haze over the pasture. The last passenger loped off to join the little knot of family waiting for him at the corner of the field. Foster Pepperidge pulled his goggles down around his neck.

"Stogie?" He hauled a new cigar out of his pocket and held it out to Ben and Dris. "Naw, I guess not." He stuck it in his own mouth, left it unlit, and talked around it. "Boys, you done a fine job. Right, Murf?"

"Sure did, Fos."

"Lessee, pulled in—" he thumbed through the wad of bills Dris had handed him "—fifty-five bucks. That's exactly right, boys. Eleven trips times five." He squinted at Dris. "I owe you something."

Dris looked blank. "I didn't ask for . . . Look, Ben, we've got to get back."

"You earned a ride, boy. Get up on that seat. Murf, give the old crock another twist."

"No," Dris said. "I'd like to, but we just don't have time. Ben, your uncle is going to . . ."

Ben gave him a hard look. Then he asked Pepperidge, as if it just slipped out, as if he hadn't been planning just how to say it, "Where do you go from here?"

"Illinois. Ain't that right, Murf? We'll try the county fairs, mebbe."

It was now or not at all, Ben realized. He blurted it out. "I wonder if you could use some help?"

The flyer rubbed his jaw with the back of his hand, and Ben saw a tremor in the grimy fingers. It could have been the strain of steady flying for almost two hours. "I'm mighty dry, Murf," Pepperidge said unexpectedly. "You got any of that . . . tonic in the automobile?"

"Fos, let's go into town for lunch." There was a peculiar pleading tone in the mechanic's voice.

"Do you think I could—" Ben began, but Pepperidge cut him off.

"Sure, sure thing. You look me up in . . . where is that place in Illinois, Murf?"

"Hughesville."

"Yeah, look me up in Hughesville. When is it, Murf?"

"Tuesday."

"Yeah, that's it. Want to thank you boys. Been a big help to us. Murf, let's get going."

"Can't we help you get the aeroplane—"

"Ben," Dris broke in, "it's way past noon! We've *got* to get back."

"Go along now," Murf insisted with an anxious glance at Pepperidge. "We got some work to do, going to take us another hour 'fore we get out of here."

"Hughesville," Ben called over his shoulder. "I'll see you there on the twenty-fifth."

"Yeah," Murf said.

Halfway back to the smithy, Dris said, "You don't really mean it, do you? To go looking for those two fellows?"

Ben gave him a tight smile. "I never meant anything so much in my life."

3

"Great God Almighty!" Alex Horner exploded. "Where have you two been! This place is wide open, nothing's been cleaned up, and Doc Miller was waiting for his shoes when I got back from town. You trying to put me out of business?"

Ben and Dris, rooted to the end of the concrete ramp leading from the street, stared up at the infuriated blacksmith. Ben knew that whatever they said would be wrong.

"It was the aeroplane, wasn't it? I knew that'd be trouble the minute the fella tried to give me that poster. He motioned with a sausagelike arm. "Get on in here and get to work. My fault as much as yours, I suppose. Can't expect boys not to take a look at an aeroplane when they get a chance."

He walked into the smithy, then turned back. "Damn, Ben, you could've at least shut the door while you were gone."

"You won't have to worry about what I do and don't do much longer," Ben said, strapping on his work apron.

"What do you mean by that?"

"I got a job with that aeroplane flyer. I'm leaving for Illinois."

Uncle Alex scowled at him, then leaned his broom against a stall door. "Dris, go around back and do some picking up." The younger boy scurried outside, and the blacksmith folded his arms and leaned back against the stall.

"Your father sent you down here for me to look after you, Ben. Don't seem to me you should go off on some harebrained goose chase six months after you get here. You learn fast and you've picked up a good bit of the business already. Few more months, and I can't call you an apprentice any more."

"I hate smithing. You know that. It's dying right out from under you. You can't even see it, can you? This is the twentieth century, and you're asking me to learn a nineteenth-century trade." Ben fought to keep his voice under control.

His uncle's reply was surprisingly gentle. "It's all I know, Ben. It's all I can teach you. That and maybe a few things about understanding people. You got quite a ways to go in that particular kind of learning, I'm afraid."

"I can take care of myself."

"I've never doubted that. It's what you do to other

31

people that bothers me. You're not a bad fella, Ben, but you don't give other people a chance to find that out."

"I look out for myself. That's the only way to get anywhere in this world."

Alex Horner gazed at him for a long moment, then he shrugged and picked up his broom. "You're the kind who has to learn by being hit over the head with life, I think. When are you planning to leave—if 'planning' is the right word?"

"Tuesday." Ben's throat went dry and he swallowed hard.

The blacksmith shook his head. "You got any money? I haven't been able to pay you much of a wage. Thought along about midsummer, I'd be able to raise you to—"

"I've got sixteen dollars," Ben put in quickly. "That'll get me to Hughesville with some to spare."

"Not much."

"I don't need much. They told me there was a job there for me."

Uncle Alex swiped his broom hard across the dirt floor. "Ben, talk in town was that those aeroplane flyers are no more than gypsies, hand-to-mouth gypsies. Flying machines are just toys for idiots to break their fool necks in. There can't be any future in that, none at all."

"Because you can't see further than a horse's hoof," Ben threw at him, "don't try to tie *me* down to this kind of life!"

His uncle's eyes glittered. "You poor bum! I'm sorry for you."

"I know you are. That's why you took me in."

The blacksmith's patience evaporated. He threw down his broom and jutted his big head forward, hands on his hips. "I took you in because I figured you could use a little help from somebody who's settled down and working hard and could be an example to you. I didn't feel sorry for you then, but, by God, I feel sorry for you now. You're mule-brained, won't listen to anybody, ready to take on the whole world to prove you're a man."

Ben picked up his hammer, swung hard, and the anvil rang. "Maybe I'm ready for that. Maybe the world just better look out."

He wasn't able to relax and sit back into the gritty day coach's green plush seat until the Wabash was a half hour behind him and the train rumbled into central Illinois. To Ben's surprise, Uncle Alex had come to the station with Dris to see him off. Dris had burned to go with Ben, but of course Dris's parents would never allow such a thing, and Dris wouldn't dare defy them. Ben didn't want him along anyway. The younger boy always seemed to hesitate just when you needed to plunge ahead.

His uncle shook hands formally. "You keep in touch with me, Ben. Letter, postcard. Let me know where you are."

As he climbed aboard, Ben opened his hand. A tightly folded twenty-dollar bill lay in his palm. He stared at the money, then back at his uncle. The big blacksmith had turned away quickly and Ben hurried into the coach.

Now he wondered for the first time if Alex Horner hadn't been right all along. The job Ben had said was waiting for him was really based on the flimsiest promise; not even a promise, Ben was forced to admit to himself. What had the bleary flyer actually said? "Look me up." And he hadn't even known the name of the place. The mechanic had to remind him.

Had Clarkston been all that bad? People had been getting to know him there, to nod to him on the street. His uncle wasn't such a hard fellow to get along with, when you thought about it. In fact, Ben had grown to admire his toughness. At least he'd always known where Uncle Alex stood on everything. Ben had begun to realize that his father had hardly ever been definite about anything.

Blacksmithing wasn't hard to learn, once you knew by its look that the white-hot forge fire was just right and got the feel of the hammer on cherry-bright strap iron. Maybe he'd made a mistake. . . . No! He forced Clarkston out of his mind and stared out the coach window.

The spring sky was clear, with just a streak of cloud along the flat horizon to the west. A good day, a good sign. The fields were hazy green with new shoots. Here and there, a late-starting farmer guided a plow behind his mule team or chugged along his acreage on a smoke-belching Fordson tractor. No matter what Uncle Alex believed, Ben thought, it's happening. Engines are here, and the horse is living his last days. Things are changing fast, and I'm going to change with them. The ka-chunk, ka-chunk of the train over the rails made him drowsy, and his head sank back against the seat.

"Hughesville!" The conductor's cry jolted Ben out of his doze. The car swayed as the brakes began to cut its speed. Telegraph poles slowed their rush past the windows. A scattering of houses drifted past, then a towering grain elevator shut out the fading afternoon sun.

The train shuddered to a stop as Ben stumbled into the aisle. He hoisted his suitcase and bumped down the steep railroad-car steps.

The air was fresh and cool after the stuffy coach, but the sun had been swallowed by a layer of thin cloud. Ben walked across the platform and peered down the wide street. A block distant, a tree-lined square sat astride the street, its white stone courthouse rising three stories above the surrounding oaks.

He walked along the uneven sidewalk and emerged in the quiet street, now seeing the big yellow general store,

Kendall's Harness Shop, a blacksmithy, hardware store, Hungerford's Dry Goods, a drugstore.

Across the way, two white clapboard churches competed for attention with the big building in the center of the town square.

Something was missing. He didn't see any posters, not a single poster advertising the mighty Conqueror of the Clouds. He frowned. There had to be a way to find out when Pepperidge was due here. Did Hughesville have a newspaper?

He found the *Clarion* office across the square, tucked in a corner next to the paint-starved Hughesville Café. The editor was a haggard horse-faced man named Appleton. Even with his permanent stoop, he was taller than Ben.

"A flyer, you say? Pepperidge? Beachey I've heard of. And Cal Rodgers, of course. But Pepperidge? Uh-uh."

"He hasn't bought any ads here? Maybe he's taken some ads you don't know about yet."

The cranelike editor slapped at a fly on the linoleum office counter. "Son, I'm editor, layout man, *and* advertising salesman for this rag. Any ad comes in, I know about it. Like to help you, but I can't." To a small man hunched over a typewriter in the back of the cluttered office, he called, "You hear of any flyer named Pepperidge coming this way, Elmo?"

"Don't think so."

"That's the best I can do for you," the newspaperman said. "Sorry."

At the marble-topped lunch counter in the Hughesville Café, Ben hunched over a bologna sandwich and coffee that tasted like mothballs. He was stunned. No Pepperidge, no job. Now what? Back to Clarkston like a little runaway kid sneaking home? Not on your life! Yet he couldn't stay here in Hughesville for no reason. He toyed

35

with his coffee spoon and watched the counterman deftly cut a cherry pie into six servings, the blunt knife thunking into the pie tin. The screen door squawked against its spring and slammed behind Elmo, the little man from the newspaper office.

"The usual for Chuck and the usual for me, Frank. I'll be taking it back to the office. Tuesday again. The *Clarion* goes to bed tonight." He noticed Ben. "Say, I thought of something after you left. Might be of some help. Might not. I heard a couple of farmers in here from Fork yesterday say there was a flyer came down over that way sometime over the weekend. Just a rumor, probably."

Ben slid off the counter stool. "Didn't you send a reporter over there to check? What kind of newspaper are you?"

"Two-man. That kind of paper. If we had a reporter, we might've sent him. But me and Chuck Appleton's got all we can handle here. Anyway, aeroplanes have landed around here before. Hardly news anymore."

The counterman slid a brown paper bag along the marble slab. "Sixty-five cents, Elmo." The man from the newspaper office slapped down a silver dollar and got his change.

"You from around here?"

"Indiana."

The little newspaperman eyed Ben's suitcase. "Passing through?"

"I came here to work. With that flyer."

"Looks like you'll have to find him first, son." Elmo picked up his bag. "Fork's a start. Twenty miles west. You got off the train too soon, but there's a milk train pulls out of here for Fork at five twenty-two. You got time to make it."

The milk train made endless stops in the waning evening

to pick up shiny cans from their railside platforms. The sky had clouded over solidly, hastening darkness and then bringing rain.

At Fork, he watched the train's lights fade into the streaming blackness. Rain pelted the wooden platform, and the few other passengers stomped off, grumbling about the weather. The small station's waiting room was dry and warm, thanks to the glow from a Franklin stove in one corner.

"Help you?" The voice came from the tiny office behind the ticket window. The station master, a red-faced man with apple cheeks, sprawled in shirt sleeves in a swivel chair, his chunky legs propped up on a table.

"Just came in from Hughesville," Ben said. "I'm looking for a flyer."

"A what?"

"A flyer. An aeroplane driver."

"Oh, him. You outta luck, fella. He come down on Arty Hamilton's place yesterday. Heard tell the machine's pretty well busted up, and that's that."

"What do you mean, 'that's that'?" Was it possible to get this close only to find disaster? "I'm going out there."

"Wouldn't in this rain. It's a good many miles. Tell you what I can do, if you don't mind sleeping a night in my barn. The missus and I'll put you up, give you breakfast, then I'll take you out to Hamilton's in my lizzie 'fore I open the station tomorrow. You come all these miles on my railroad, least I can do is get you the last bit of the way."

The ride eight miles north to the Hamilton farm just after sunrise took almost an hour. The sun had broken through pink clouds, but more than a few minutes of new heat would be needed to harden the dirt road that last night's rain had melted into three-inch-deep mud in the low spots. The Ford skidded and bucked, but it took more than mud to halt a tin lizzie. Around seven, they pulled into a collection of ramshackle buildings badly in need of paint.

A thin, ancient farmer in tattered overalls peered at them from the open barn door. Then he recognized the driver and waved a clawlike hand.

"Got a long-distance traveler to see the flyer," the stationmaster called to spidery Arty Hamilton.

"Ain't going to see him here, Newton," the old farmer threw back at him as he walked to the car on bowed legs. "He's gone. Aeroplane's here. Mechanic's here. Flyer's gone."

"That so?"

"Yup. Come in here with his motor rattling like a can of rocks. Set down in my east pasture. Sixty-rod field, but he only used a corner of it. Stood the machine right on its danged snoot. Mechanic rattled in here by lizzie right after that, and the flyer took the lizzie and disappeared. Mechanic's been moping around like a sick pup ever since."

At that point, a red-haired skeleton in floppy coveralls loped around a corner of the barn, then stopped short. "Heck," he muttered. "Thought you was Fos. Should of knowed better by now."

Ben recognized Pepperidge's mechanic, Murf, who ambled slowly to the auto. "Ain't I seen you somewheres before?" Murf asked him.

"In Indiana, a few days ago. I sold rides for you in Clarkston."

Murf's bony face broke into a yellow-toothed grin. "Bells afire! What're you doing in this neck of the woods, boy?"

"The job Pepperidge promised me," Ben said, confused. "He said to come to Hughesville. I was there, but he wasn't. Then I went to Fork, and the stationmaster brought—"

"Clarkston." Murf rubbed his long jaw. "Oh, yeah, I remember him saying . . . Well, long's you're here, might's well see what happened to the old birdcage."

"There *is* a job?"

"Machine's down here past the barn," Murf said a little too quickly.

Out in the pasture beyond the barn, the Wright rested on its four wheels, but the skids were badly split at their tips. Their supporting braces had carried the shock of the nose-down landing to the center of the top wing. The linen covering was wrinkled and torn. "Busted some wing ribs, too," Murf said. "She can be fixed. Anything made of wood, wire, and cloth can be fixed. But Fos ain't come back with the stuff to do it with. Been gone since yesterday."

The stationmaster plodded around the stricken biplane, kicked a tire and shrugged. "So that's an airyplane! First I ever saw. Don't really look like much."

"Don't plow fields, don't plant corn, don't even fly when the wind's at all stiff," Hamilton joined in. "That's why it's here. Come down to get out of the wind and knocked its snoot right into the ground."

The railroader walked back to them, his shoes leaving depressions in the soft sod. "You want to come back to Fork with me or what?" he asked Ben. "Ain't nothing here for you, I reckon."

"The aeroplane's here," Ben said. "That's why I came."

The apple-cheeked stationmaster stuck out his lower lip, then spit thoughtfully. "You get around Fork again, drop in and say howdy. Arty, looks like he's all yours. Going to have a crowd around here."

"Like blazes, Newton! Sooner everybody gets out of here, the quicker. This is a dairy farm, not a cussed flying field. I got work to do. Get your aeroplane out of here soon's you can," he snapped at Murf. "You're making a pig wallow out of my cow pasture!" He stomped off to see Newton back to his Ford.

Ben watched them disappear around the corner of the barn. "Hamilton's a charmer, isn't he?"

"Oh, he ain't bad," Murf said. "We did mess up his pasture some. I figure he's getting a boot outa all this, but he's lived alone fer so long, he's forgot how to talk to folks." The bean-pole mechanic leaned against the lower wing and chewed his tobacco cud.

"If I had any brains at all, I'da stayed in the auto-racing business. Woulda made Fos stay in it, too. But no. 'Edgar Murfine,' he says, 'I'll show you how to make some real money. Flying machines are the wave of the future.' Some wave! Ain't made a ripple yet. Just struggling from town to town. Buck here, buck there. What real money? Bells afire, there wouldn't be any real money in this even if Fos didn't go off alla time and—" He stopped and eyed Ben. "Ferget that. Just haven't had anybody to talk to 'cept that crusty old buzzard, Hamilton. Why're you sticking around here, boy?"

Ben ignored the question. "Where is Pepperidge?"

"Took the Model T and went over to Claxton for some spruce wood and linen cloth."

"How far is this Claxton?"

"Maybe ten, maybe twelve miles. What's the difference?"

"He's been gone nearly two days," Ben said. "What's really wrong?"

"What the heck you mean, 'what's really wrong'? He just ain't come back yet."

"Why?" Ben insisted.

Murf met his eyes for a long moment, then he dropped his gaze to the ground and spit at a mud clod. "Ah, the heck with it. I'm tired of coverin' up for him. What's the difference, anyway? He's a boozer, kid. On the sauce. Good as gold for a stretch, then something goes wrong and he's off on a toot for mebbe a whole week. Like now. Come in here 'cause the wind was about to tear him apart on the way to Hughesville. Put the Wright out of commission, and that was all it took. Bells afire, he was heading for this toot when you seen him in Clarkston."

He bent down and snatched at a stalk of foxtail grass. "Gets to walking sort of stiff-legged and staring at the sky over your head. That's the start of it. Then it's a reg'lar rolly coaster. Few more snorts and he's gone. Stuff's poison to him. But when he comes out of it, you'd never know anything happened. Enough to drive you nuts, working with him. But it's kind of sad, too, if you know what I mean."

He pushed away from the edge of the wing with his elbows. "What can I do? Just have to wait him out. He shows up if I wait long enough."

Anger had been building inside Ben. Now it boiled over. It was bad enough to come all this distance, to put in all this effort just to learn Foster Pepperidge wouldn't even remember talking to him in Clarkston. But it was even more infuriating to see Murf wandering around, hands in his pockets, kicking at dirt clods and not doing anything about this mess!

"This is stupid!" he snapped. "You're standing here like you can't do anything without him. What's the matter with you?"

Murf was taken aback. "What *can* I do?"

"We can both get ourselves over to Claxton and drag Pepperidge back here. That's what we can do."

Murf bit his lower lip. "I guess that is better than this." Then he seemed to come to sudden life. "Yeah! We'll get that flying rumhound back out here if we have to set his tail on fire—" He stopped. "Wait a minute. How are we going to get to Claxton?"

Ben pulled out his wallet and waved it under Murf's long nose. "Hamilton has an auto. I saw it in the barn. He'll rent it to us, or Pepperidge can give him a free ride in the Wright when he sobers up."

"Or maybe before he sobers up," Murf said with an unexpected grin. "He was drunk when he took you up, and you thought he was great!"

Hamilton let them have his battered old KisselKar for two dollars plus Murf's inspired promise to tune it at no charge and fix the miss it had developed months before. When he had driven them only a quarter mile, Murf stomped on the brakes, leaped out and opened the hood. "Bells afire, that's an easy one! Plug lead's loose." He clamped the hood back in place and climbed aboard again. "Hang on, boy. Claxton, here we come!"

The KisselKar backfired, blasting a glob of soot against the bright sunset behind them. Then all thirty horses howled as they hurtled down the gravel county road toward Claxton and Foster Pepperidge.

4

In size, Ben observed from the high seat of the chugging KisselKar, Claxton was midway between Hughesville and Fork. The town lacked Hughesville's central square, but its streets were a long step up from Fork's hard-packed dirt. Claxton's were paved with tarred gravel. The town had something neither of the other two burgs had at all: two barrooms right on the main street and another in the ramshackle Hotel Clax. There was even more brassy clangor at the far end of the street, where a fair-sized carnival was being unloaded at the rail depot.

They parked behind a dilapidated buggy with a skittish horse, then checked the bars.

"Flyer? He was in here last night," one of the shirt-sleeved bartenders told them. "But I ain't seen him today."

"Probably in the hotel," Murf guessed. "You wait here with the machine."

"I'm going with you."

Murf gave Ben a quick look, then shrugged. "If you think you gotta."

They crossed the tiled lobby, where several traveling salesmen were noisily escorting an assortment of hard-looking women into the dining room beyond the lobby's dusty potted palms.

"You got a Foster Pepperidge registered?" Murf asked the desk clerk. "Little fella with hair like a whisk broom. Flyer."

"Oh, the flyer." The pudding-faced clerk eyed Murf's stained coveralls. "You from the carnival?"

"Bells afire, man! I'm his mechanic."

The clerk pulled off his rimless pince-nez with a thumb and forefinger and pursed his lips. "I don't know . . ."

"If I don't find him, you ain't gonna get paid. I handle the money."

"Oh, it's like that. Well, he's in two sixteen. Been there since yesterday."

They clumped up the stairs behind the registration desk alcove and followed the room numbers down the hallway. The walls needed paint, and the runner was faded and patched. Murf rapped on the door of 216. Silence. He rapped again.

"G'way!" The voice was thick and raspy.

"Open it or we'll bust it in!" Ben said loudly.

"Who's out there? Who is that?"

"It's me, Fos," Murf called. "Me and that fella helped us at Clarkston."

44

"Don't know anybody from Clars . . . Clarstown. Never been in Clarstown."

"Yes, we were. Few days ago. Come on, Fos, open the door and let's get moving."

"Why should I?"

" 'Cause we'll never get the aeroplane out of Hamilton's pasture if you don't, that's why."

"Never get it out, anyway. My head's bigger'n a Baldwin balloon. Never get my head off the ground, let alone a whole flying machine."

Murf groaned. "We ain't getting anywhere."

"Well, we're going to get somewhere," Ben announced. "I'll get him out." His shoe crashed against the door, a deafening blow in the narrow hall.

"Holy Saint Jake!" Pepperidge exploded. "You're trying to kill me!"

"Open the door." Ben's voice was hard. His foot hit the panel again. "I can keep this up all night, Pepperidge, and I will."

"Holy moley, boy! You're going to murder me right here in bed. I've flown in near every state east of the Mississippi and never got a scratch on me. Now you're going to kill me with noise."

Between the slams of Ben's shoe, they heard mutterings. Then a key rattled and the door opened a crack. In the weak glow of the hall bulb, Foster Pepperidge was the color of curdled cream. His eyes were red-edged and baggy. His hair was like a wheat shock after a wind squall, and apparently he hadn't shaved for two days. "I'll be out." His breath drove them back a yard. "Jus' cut out that fritterin' noise!" The watery eyes wavered toward the ceiling. He began to shut the door on them, but Ben slid his shoe against it.

"The heck with that. You're coming with us right now."

Pepperidge pulled his eyes off the ceiling and squinted. "Who the devil are you, sonny?"

"Clarkston," Murf threw in quickly. "I told you, Fos."

"No kid's going to order me around, Clarstown or no Clarstown."

But Ben was already inside, searching for the light toggle. The overhead bulb flooded the room with a glare that blinded them all. Ben made out a battered chest of drawers, two scarred chairs, and a metal bed with chipped ivory enamel that hadn't felt a paintbrush in years. The bed was a tangle of gray sheets and washed-out blue blankets.

Fos stood in the center of the room in the bottom half of his two-piece long johns, naked from the waist up. He wobbled and tried to get his eyes to focus. "Anything left in that bottle, Murf?"

Murf beat him to the bourbon bottle on the floor near the bed. He dropped it into the metal wastebasket with an ear-shattering crash. "There's nothing good in any bottle for you, Fos. Get dressed. We've got a lot of work to do, and then we're going to make some real money, right?"

"Uh-huh. Yeah. Right."

"Here's your britches," Murf offered. "Can you handle 'em by yourself?"

Fos rocked on one leg, then grabbed Murf's shoulder. "Almost, Murf. Little rocky. Jus' little rocky."

Ben began to laugh. It really was funny, the half-naked flyer and his gangling mechanic trying to solve the riddle of a twisted pair of riding breeches. It was funny until Murf looked up at him, and Ben saw the anguish in his face.

"Ben, he's going to kill hisself," Murf said when they had returned to Hamilton's place. After their rescue of the flyer, it was "Ben," no longer "boy." Fos had wobbled off to

46

the extra bedroom the old farmer had agreed they could use for a dollar a night. Cocky after his one driving lesson in the Studebaker a few days ago, Ben had driven the Ford that Pepperidge had taken to Claxton. Now he sprawled on the front porch with Murf. The mechanic bit off a chunk of chewing tobacco from an evil-looking plug he kept in a coverall pocket.

"Use this?"

"No, thanks." Ben leaned against a square porch pillar. The air was still and the soft darkness carried the pungent smell of cows in their stalls. Ben's drive from Claxton had been something he wouldn't forget for a while. The hard-cranking, jackrabbiting tin lizzie hadn't been anything like the Studebaker. His one lesson hadn't really qualified him for the struggle to follow the bobbing taillight of the KisselKar along the rutted horse road from Claxton back to the farm, but he'd managed.

He clasped his hands around his upraised knee and looked up at the stars between wisps of scud cloud. "You think Pepperidge is going to drink himself to death?"

"Drink hisself to death? I said he's going to kill hisself. Maybe booze, but probably flying into a tree he don't see some morning after a toot. Either way, he ain't going to get to be a real old man."

"Can't he see that? Why does he keep pouring it down?"

"Dunno. Nobody knows the answer to that one. Preacher'd say the devil's in him, but that's hogwash. It's a sickness. He don't want to do it, but when the thirst hits him, he can't help hisself."

"He always been like this?"

"Since I knowed him. Before that, I suppose. It ain't the kind of thing you ask a fella about, is it?"

"Where'd Pepperidge come from? He's got some kind of accent, then again, he doesn't."

"Canada. Told me his folks went from England to Montreal to work for some big family there. Then they got tired of cooking and gardening for somebody else, so they bought a place in Ontario. By the time he was twenty or so, Fos got tired of hanging on to a plow. He left and worked around horse tracks in New York State."

Murf shifted his tobacco and fired a quick squirt into the darkness off the end of the porch. "When they began racing autos at the tracks, he got into that and started working the circuit as a race driver. Buicks, Locomobiles, Fiats, Marmons. I ran into him when I was fixing racers in Ohio. Youngstown. That's where I'm from."

"If he was a race driver and you were an auto mechanic, how did you both end up with an aeroplane?"

"Oh, one Sunday he signed up to race a Marmon against some character flying a Curtiss. Well, from that day when the Curtiss beat him, Fos wasn't going to be happy till he got to be a flyer, hisself. Begged lessons, even bought lessons when there wasn't no other way. He finally made it, and we put every buck we owned into that old Model B Wright."

That was a surprise. "You both own it?"

"Yep."

"But you never fly it."

"Bells afire, Ben, I'm a mechanic, not a flyer."

Ben decided not to press the point. "You said he was drinking like this when you met him?"

Murf's jaws worked the tobacco. "First time I saw it was in Delaware. Smyrna. Had a bad day there. Didn't make beans. Quit flying just 'fore dark, tied the machine down, then Fos 'vaporated. I didn't know what to do, so I waited in that hay field. Slept under the wings, got a few meals at a farmhouse down the road. Then, when I'd decided he'd fell in a hole and died someplace, there he came, stumbling over the rise, all bloody-eyed and whisker-chinned, like now. 'Where you been?' I ask him. 'In town,' he says. 'For three days?' I ask. Then he breaks down right in front of me. 'It's something I can't help, Murf. Just can't do nothing about it. Booze gets holda me and I just got to drink it off. Like a fritterin' sickness I can't get rid of,' he says. Well, from that day, I never said no more 'bout it. Never went after him, neither. Not till tonight."

Hamilton's barn had half a second story, reached by ladder and used for hay storage. Another night in a barn, Ben thought, but the barns are getting bigger. That didn't mean things were getting better, though. He'd found Pepperidge and the flyer turned out to be a drunk. The machine was smacked up, and nobody seemed to know when it could be fixed.

He tossed his cap aside, rolled up his jacket for a pillow, and tried to wipe his mind blank. But he had a hard time getting to sleep. The whole calamity kept running through his brain over and over again like a bad dream.

The stamping and snorting of cattle on the ground floor woke him at daylight. Arty Hamilton was driving his black-and-white Holsteins out to pasture. Ben yawned, stretched his stiff muscles, and climbed down the loft ladder.

"Want to cook yourself some eggs, go on up to the kitchen, but mind you clean up after," Hamilton grumbled.

To Ben's surprise, Pepperidge and Murf were already in the kitchen, and Murf was scrambling a huge pan of eggs and beans.

"Scrambled beans?"

"Take what you can get," Murf advised. "In the flying business, it can be a long time between meals."

Ben stole a glance at Pepperidge, hunched over his coffee mug at the table in the middle of the big farm kitchen. "You feeling better?"

"Me, boy? Why not? Man's entitled to a night out once in a while, ain't he? I'm fit as a fiddle and ready to get that old birdcage back on its way to Hughesville."

So that took care of Pepperidge's two-day drunk. A snap of the fingers and it was over.

But something else was unresolved. "Mr. Pepperidge, about the job you—"

"Blang it, boy! You seen me at my worst and I think that gives you the right to call me Fos."

"Well, okay then, Fos. About the job you promised me in Clarkston . . ."

"You know, I can't 'member a fritterin' thing about Clarkston. I swear, my memory is getting so it ain't worth the powder blown to pot. What'd you say I did there?"

"Promised me a job."

"Doing what? There ain't enough money in what we do to keep me and Murf and the aeroplane alive, let alone take on another mouth. I guess I ought to thank you for helping to drag me out of Claxton, but you can see for yourself how rich Murf and me are getting, holed in here with the Wright all busted up."

"I gave up a job to come out here on a promise you don't even remember. I spent my own money to get you out of Claxton. I'd say you owe me."

"That right, Murf?"

The mechanic nodded. "Paid your hotel bill. Paid Hamilton for the auto rent. Fact is, now we're eating and sleeping on his money."

"And I made money for you back in Indiana," Ben put in. He had an advantage now, and he wasn't going to let it cool off.

"Like the fella says. He and his friend sold more'n fifty bucks worth of rides that day, Fos."

Fos squinted at Ben with watery eyes. "You willing to work on straight commission? Say ten percent of whatever we take in?"

Ben's heart thudded. It was happening, really happening!

"And pay your own keep," Fos threw in quickly.

"A deal!" Ben reached across the table and grabbed Fos's skinny hand. "Hughesville, here we come!"

"Whoa! Wait a minute. We ain't got no aeroplane to fly, 'member?"

"But we got extra help now, Fos," Murf pointed out.

"What's he know 'bout flying machines, Murf? He's just a green kid."

"I learn fast," Ben said. "I've already got a tenth of your business."

Fos glared at him, then broke into a shout of cackling laughter. "Holy Saint Jake! You're all right, kid. I got a feeling you can do 'bout anything you say you can. You think we can get that old birdcage back in the air, let's get at it!"

On Monday, Ben had an inspiration, but Fos wasn't sold on it. "I dunno, Ben. I dunno." After four days of struggling on the big repair job side by side with his new partner, Fos no longer called him "boy" or "kid."

"I dunno," he repeated. "We got a pack of posters a fella made up for us in Ohio. Got a blank space on the bottom where Murf marks in the time and place. We never tried no other way of advertising."

"That's just it," Ben pressed. "You've got to do more. Those posters are all right, but that's only part of it. I think you're missing out on a lot of free publicity. Don't you ever go to the newspapers and get them to put in a story about you?"

"What do we know about newspapers? What do you know about newspapers, come to think of it?"

"I know the Hughesville *Clarion* gets put together on Tuesdays. I know where and by whom. That ought to be enough for a start. You sure you can be in Hughesville this week?"

"Everything that could go wrong has gone wrong, blang it. Radiator blew on us Saturday. Water in the gas yesterday. There's nothing left to bust. I'll be there."

"Make sure you are, Fos, because if you don't show up, I'll be the guy they'll go after. I'm going to Hughesville tomorrow. I'll find a good field and mark it with a white *X* so you can find it from the air. No, wait a minute. I'll mark it with a *T*."

"Why a *T*?"

"Because anybody'd expect an *X* as a marker. Let's let them wonder about the *T*."

Fos chuckled. "Could stand for 'This is the place.'"

"Or 'Tip it over here,'" Ben offered.

"Sure hope not. Another landing like I made here, and we'll starve to death sure." Fos pulled a cigar out of his shirt pocket and puffed hard against the match. "You still got some money? Murf'll take you to the train in Fork. You carry a supply of them posters along. Fill them in and get them up. I ain't all that sure 'bout your newspaper idea. Let's set the time for two o'clock Sunday afternoon."

Hughesville's square seemed familiar now. As Ben walked in from the rail depot at dusk, another idea came to him.

"I found the missing flyer!" he shouted as he banged into the newspaper office. "Crashed north of Fork. He was on his way here, but he didn't make it. Went down in a rainstorm last—"

"Crashed?" Chuck Appleton stopped in midstride like a big coonhound who had just found a live scent. "The devil you say! Anybody hurt? Anybody *killed?*"

He was hooked!

"That flyer was mighty lucky this time. But it's taken him a week to fix the machine. The wind got him, knocked him right out of the air."

"Elmo, take notes, take notes. Where'd this happen? Who's the driver? How much damage?"

The story was a full column on the *Clarion*'s front page the next morning. Along with it, Ben had gotten his armload of posters imprinted free. After a night of impatient tossing in the rooming house Chuck Appleton had mentioned, he rented a sturdy Elgin King from the Hughesville Cycle Shop. By noon, he had found a flat, well-mowed hayfield along a stretch of county road, made a deal with the owner for a ten-dollar use fee—payable Sunday—and pedaled the Elgin four miles back to town.

The posters were up by midafternoon. In an hour, Ben found that he had become a minor celebrity himself. A straw-hatted man came up behind him as he tacked the last poster to a telephone pole. "This Pepperidge do the Death Dip like Beachey? How many times he crashed?"

How could he answer stuff like that? Ben wondered. Fos wasn't any stunting flyer. "Daring Aeronaut" Foster Pepperidge wasn't any more a Conqueror of the Clouds than Ben was a champion six-day bike racer.

"I don't know how many times he's crashed." The man gave him a sour look. "That's because he's lost count," Ben added quickly.

That went over better. These rubes would never be able to check up on what he said. What was he worried about?

"Sure, he's done the Death Dip, but so many ladies fainted that he doesn't try it too often."

The little knot that had gathered around Ben on Center Street grew into a cluster. "Hey, fella," the aproned proprietor of the general store called, "come on up here for a Moxie on the house."

Ben moved his circle of gaping citizens to the wooden steps. He took a swig of the tart, heavy-tasting stuff. "I've never seen Beachey fly, but Pepperidge has plenty of tricks up his own sleeve."

"Got a cousin in Los Angeles," announced a man built like a slick-haired Jim Jeffries, pushing free of his porch pillar to get his arms into action. An iceman, Ben guessed; he still wore his leather shoulder guard. "This cousin of mine seen Arch Hoxsey get killed in 1910. Couple days after Christmas. Hoxsey was trying to beat his own record for high flying. Took him more'n an hour to get up maybe seven thousand feet, Ev told me, then it looked like he give up. Come back down in a long curve, then he begin to swoop down and back up, swish, swish. . . ." He made long dips with his hands, thumbs locked together.

"Then Ev said Hoxsey turned the machine on its side maybe five hundred feet up. Gust of wind got him. She broke up right in midair. Whole thing come down like a rock. Smashed Hoxsey to pulp, Ev said. 'Nough to make you sick."

"Yeah? Yeah?" the crowd muttered eagerly. They didn't sound sick, Ben noticed. He had to get their attention back.

"Pepperidge has had plenty of close ones," he announced loudly, "but he's a slick flyer. A mighty slick flyer. You'll see when you come out to Bailer's place Sunday."

"You sure he's gonna put on a good show?" the big iceman challenged. "A bunch of us was planning to go on over to Claxton that day, see that carnival. They're gonna shoot come fathead out of a cannon!"

"That so?" someone said in an excited yip. "What time's that to be, Ivan?"

" 'Bout the same time this flying fella's due over to Andy Bailer's."

"Can't make 'em both. Anybody ever seen someone shot out of a cannon?"

"I have," Ben said truthfully.

"Yeah? Where?"

"Indianapolis." His father had taken him the twenty miles on the train. In the hot tent, the drumroll had been endless, the sudden silence unbearable. The slam of the cannon had shaken his belly. "It's a fake," Ben said. "A spring pushes the guy out. The explosion is just a sound effect."

"Yeah, but my Gawd, what happens then?"

Ben remembered the slim white-clad body streaking through the smoke from the cannon's huge mouth, soaring high above the center ring, arching down, the crowd sound melting into a long "Ahhh . . . !" "He just lands in a net. It only lasts maybe five seconds altogether." How had he gotten into this verbal contest between Fos and some idiot stunt man?

"Where you going Sunday, Ivan?" asked a little fellow with rimless glasses and a drooping blond moustache.

The ice hauler glowered at Ben. "Sure hate to pass up that nut in the cannon."

Ben chewed his lower lip. How far did he dare go?

"Yeah, Ivan, I'm with you," said a bullet-headed farmer in faded overalls. "We'll have other chances to see aeroplane drivers."

They were getting away just when he'd had them in the palm of his hand. He had to do something and do it quickly. "Wait a minute! You'll never see another flyer like Foster Pepperidge. I haven't told you about his . . . his specialty."

That got them. "What specialty, boy?"

"What's he do? What's he do?"

"You'll have to see it to believe it. What he does is . . . indescribable." Amazing how easy it was to string these people along. "That's right. Nobody who's seen it has ever been able to tell it right."

Big Ivan stepped close to Ben and glared into his face. "If you're faking, fella, you'll wish to blazes you never heered of Hughesville!"

"Dern tootin', Ivan. We're all with you. If he's lying, we'll give him something to fly with all right!"

"Yep!" yelled a sour-looking character. "Feathers!"

"With plenty of tar to stick 'em on good and tight!"

They broke into a roar of laughter that made the warm afternoon suddenly chilly. When Ben finally got away and, after a sandwich at the Hughesville Café, was bedded down in the rooming house, he couldn't sleep, not with his ridiculous promises tumbling through his head. The citizens of Hughesville wouldn't get a chance to lynch him. Foster Pepperidge would do it for them.

5

Fos yanked his sodden cigar out of his mouth and threw it to the ground. " 'Specialty'! Holy Saint Jake, Ben, my specialty is carrying passengers at five bucks a head. I don't know any tricks. Fact is, I spend part of my time up there just praying that the old bucket won't fall apart flying in a straight line. Now you want me to do some kind of fancy-Dan flying. Not me, Ben. No, sirree."

"I'm only asking you to live up to your poster. It says you're a daring aeronaut. 'Conqueror of the Clouds.' "

Fos grunted. "Told you that dang poster of yours'd get me in trouble one day," he said to Murf. "Well, this ain't gonna be the day."

"You don't have a choice," Ben said without sympathy.

"I talked these people into coming here instead of to the carnival in Claxton. The only way I could do that was promise them a better show here."

"You shouldna."

"We'd be all alone out here if I hadn't."

A hundred feet across the hay field, near the road, a froggy voice shouted out of the crowd. "Awright, show us what we come fer. Else they's gonna be a whale of a lot of upset people around here."

"Yeah, you tell 'em, Herm! Let's see something to beat that cannon-shooter fella." Ben recognized that second voice. Ivan the iceman. The crowd along the county roadside broke into impatient yelling.

Ben lost his own patience. "Look, Fos, you can fake some kind of—"

"Of what?" Fos burst out. "Just what would you like me to do? Kill myself? That's what would make these gopher chasers happy."

"Just do something that *looks* dangerous," Ben urged.

"Bells afire, Ben, anything that looks dangerous in that old box kite *is* dangerous," Murf offered.

"Some partner," Fos muttered. "Everything was going along more or less easy till you come by."

"Easy!" Ben shot back. "You two weren't making enough money to buy gas with when I got here. Your aeroplane was busted up and you were in Claxton with a bot——"

Fos waved a hand. "Awright, Ben, awright. We all make mistakes. The best thing to do now is figger how we can get out of this one."

From the edge of the field, the iceman's heavy voice boomed, "Get going, birdman. 'Fore we give you some extra feathers!" An ominous cackle of laughter rose from the spectators.

Close to two hundred people had driven autos, pedaled bikes, or walked out here from Hughesville. Fos should at least thank him for getting this many people together, Ben thought sourly.

The flyer ran a nervous hand through his wheat-shock hair. "I been noticing them trees 'cross the other side of the field. Mighty tall stand of sycamores, and they come clear around the west side, too." He scratched an ear and squinted into the afternoon sunlight. The sycamores wavered in the heat rising off the field. "Let's get at it," Fos said with sudden assurance.

The Wright clattered away across the field's hummocks, its twin propeller disks shimmering. A smell of scalded oil filled the air in its wake. The tree line threw the engine's rasp back at them, and Murf said, "Sounds like she may live. Better'n I thought she'd sound, considering we siphoned the gas outta Hamilton's KisselKar."

The aeroplane rose above a cloud of old hay clippings, banked and climbed. The cluster of people from Hughesville shaded their eyes and followed the biplane's rise.

"So what's he going to do?"

"Dunno, Ben," Murf shrugged. "You saw him. Just stuck a cigar in his mouth and told me to start the machine."

The Wright was tiny in the distance and far higher than Ben had seen it over Clarkston.

"He should be closer," he said. "You can't see much from here."

"He's turning. Coming back. Must be up a thousand feet!"

The biplane rattled toward them, now racing downwind.

"Sounds awright," Murf said, "but I got all ten fingers crossed."

The engine popped twice and died. The Wright pitched forward. Wind began to wail through its maze of struts, an eerie rising shriek that made the hairs on Ben's neck stand up.

"Bells afire!" Murf gasped. "That KisselKar gas . . ."

The Wright plunged close to vertical. The wind tore through its struts and wires in a scream. Ben's palms grew wet. He'd never expected a disaster like this. The stupid crowd was going to get more than it came for!

"It's more'n engine trouble!" Murf's voice was shrill. "She'd sail pretty good without power. Control wire musta busted at the same time. Come on, Fos, straighten her up!" he shouted through cupped hands. *"Straighten her up!"*

The Wright flashed down behind the sycamores. Its death howl chopped off. From the crowd came an animal noise. "Aaaah!" Then the growl was shot through with female shrieks, like fingernails on slate. They broke into a stampede, all two hundred of them, and streamed across the hay field like a pack of hounds who had just gotten a good look at the fox. They pounded past Ben and Murf, shoved them aside, gulped air between shouts, their faces twisted with the unbelievable excitement of it all.

"They'll tear everything to bits fer souvenirs," Murf cried. "Won't be nothing left to bury!"

They raced after the mob, pushed stragglers aside, and sprinted through the middle of the crush. Then an ear-blasting roar broke behind them. Ben whirled—and stared straight into the front of the Wright, not a hundred feet away. Its broad wings were huge. Fos hunched forward on the lower wing perch, his unlit cigar jutting straight into the wind. The four landing wheels ticked the new grass.

The crowd swung around, faces frozen in their eagerness

to see the kill. Then they broke, threw themselves flat, dived facedown, pitched over sideways, anything to get away from the supposedly dead aeroplane that had miraculously snarled back to life.

A pudgy man backpedaled furiously, then fell flat on his broad bottom. Iceman Ivan leaped sideways, fell over his own big feet, and threw his arms over his head.

The Wright stormed past, its wash tossing the skirts of the prostrate women. The engine's roar rolled past them and on down the field. The harsh smell of burned castor oil and rusty water boiled in the air. The aeroplane rose, swung around to meet the wind, and settled in a hundred yards away. The propeller shimmers broke into sticks, then the propellers clanked silent.

Fos's voice came thinly across the field. "All right, you vultures, you got your thrill. Now let's have some passengers!"

"Not me," said a heronlike man in blue denim, brushing off the dust from his dive to the turf. "Way that motor cut out on him, I wouldn't get in that thing if he paid me!"

"You dumb bunnies!" Ben yelled in exasperation. The whole thing was so obvious now. "It was a trick. He cut the power himself, dived behind the trees where we couldn't see him, then he swung around behind us."

"I know what my own eyes saw, boy. Nobody here's gonna take a chance on that thing. Ferget it!" The rest of the crowd was already heading for the road. In five minutes there was only a thin trail of settling dust.

Ben stood in front of the Wright, his fingers wrapped around one of its varnished struts, and watched the last distant auto jounce toward town. Fos and Murf squatted on the ground. Murf reached into his coveralls for his Granger plug. "I guess that just 'bout does it," he muttered. "We'll have to scratch up the ten bucks field rent between us for Bailey or whatever his name is. Today was a real bust. Yessir, a real hog-tied bells-afire bust."

"I got you a crowd," Ben pointed out. "That's what you wanted."

Fos shrugged. "Probably the biggest crowd we ever had. But what good was it?"

"Flying passengers wasn't doing much for you. I think I was right in trying something else."

"But the 'something else' finished off our passenger business altogether."

"That wasn't the mistake," Ben said. "We had what they wanted. To be excited. To be scared. That's what they wanted." Sudden realization hit him. "No one was mad today because we scared them. They just didn't want to fly in the machine that scared them."

Fos squinted at him. "What're you driving at, Ben?"

"You gave a free show today. I think they would have paid for it. It's stupid to get a crowd together, then try to sell rides to just some of them, specially if you put on a show to get the crowd together to begin with." He snapped his fingers. "I've got it! What we should sell is the *show*. And to all of them!"

Fos shook his head. "I ain't no aerobat flyer, Ben. I was scared near to death when I cut that engine and dived down behind them sycamores. I never come down that steep before. And them turns close to the ground so's I could swing around behind everybody—gives me goosey bumps just talking 'bout it. No, I ain't no trick flyer. Not me."

"But you were a race driver," Ben said. "That's not such a safe way to make a living, is it?"

"It's not the same. I get into a tight spot in an auto race, that was one thing. Up in the air, something happens to me." Fos hunched forward. "Different, that's all."

"I know I'm right," Ben insisted. "We have to sell the show, not the rides. I could have sold tickets to every one of them today just to watch."

"No, you couldn't," Murf put in. "They could've seen it whether they paid or not. You gotta do a show someplace where it's set up for that kind of business. A fair or something."

"Or a carnival!" Ben said. "Like that one in Claxton. What we have to do is work out a routine that's done right in front of the crowd, so every rubbernecker can't just stand a mile away and get a free look."

"Ain't going to do it," Fos insisted. "I'm a passenger flyer, not a powder-blown-to-pot stunt man. It takes a certain kind of nut to be a trick flyer. I ain't that kind."

Murf said, "Nobody's down on you 'cause of the kind of flying you do, Fos. Man's a man, right, Ben? What he likes or don't like to do, that's his business."

"Then I don't see what we can do other than go on like we been, Murf. I ain't gonna fly no circus tricks." Fos stood up. "Best we split up here and now, Ben, 'fore any more damage is done. Some way or other, we'll pay you back the money of yours we spent. You leave us an address. Sorry how things are, but there ain't no other way."

"Yes, there is." Ben had been thinking it over since they had begun talking, and now the daring of it nearly took his breath away.

Fos cocked his head at him. "Like what?"

"Teach me to fly the Wright. I'll be your trick aviator."

6

Perched in the front seat of the lizzie, Fos grumbled all the way to Claxton. But as Ben pointed out, there was no better way to get into the aeroplane show business.

"I dunno, Ben. Seems to me you're pushing us mighty hard into something we got no business being in."

"If we don't try it, we'll be in no business at all," Ben countered from the jouncing rear seat.

"What do you think, Murf?" Fos asked for the fifth time.

The mechanic wrestled the Model T around a soft spot in the roadway. " 'Fraid Ben's hard to argue with at this point, Fos. We ain't got but seven bucks amongst us."

They found Lucien Rathrock, the carnival operator, sitting at the foot of the steps to his office wagon, saddle-soaping a pair of worn cavalry boots. He listened to Ben's proposition without looking up.

"An aeroplane? Never heard of a carnival with an aeroplane. Interests me some." He dabbed saddle soap on a boot toe. "Just some."

"We can work on a commission setup," Ben urged, hoping he didn't sound too anxious.

"Could," Rathrock said without looking up, "could." He set down his boots and straightened. "Let me lay it right on the line, gents. My average take has been three hundred a weeknight, double that on Friday nights and Saturdays. Triple on Sundays, when the human cannonball flies. I'll give you, say, twenty percent of every dollar over those base figures."

"Say twenty-fi——" Fos began.

"Say a third," Ben interrupted.

"You're pushing me mighty close to the line, gents." Rathrock was a broad sweaty-faced man with a left eye that kept winking on its own. They had trouble deciding whether the barrel-shaped carnival owner standing in front of his business wagon in his shirt sleeves and cowboy hat was serious or pulling legs with that washed-out blue eye winking on and on.

"Somewhere along the way, I got to make a buck, too," he protested.

"Two thirds of something is better than three thirds of nothing," Ben tossed back.

"Con men and crooks is all I ever get to deal with these days," Rathrock muttered. "Con men and crooks. Okay, okay, shave it a couple percents and you're on. A fat lot of good it'll be to me, though, at those robber rates of yours, kid."

They took the deal at thirty percent, not quite the third Ben had asked, but more than Lucien Rathrock had originally offered. They never would know how high he really had been willing to go, but eventually they would learn that the human cannonball was working a fifty percent Sunday cut. Of course, he performed behind high canvas screening and every gawker was a paid admission.

Ben's first flying lesson was the flight to the Claxton fairgrounds from Hughesville the day after they made the deal with Rathrock. Fos, in the passenger seat, coaxed the old Wright out of the hay field using the dual controls, then he spent the next twenty minutes shouting at Ben's panicky leaps and swerves. The controls made no sense to Ben at all. Fos kept grabbing the wing warping lever out of Ben's right hand to yank the machine back on course. His screech cut across the engine's bark. "Fritterin' lunkhead! You fly like a pig farmer!"

When Fos finally clumped them down on the fairgrounds, Ben stared straight ahead while the engine's hot metal clinked behind them and smelled of old oil. Then Fos nearly knocked him out of the seat with: "Wasn't too bad, Ben. Just takes practice."

On his second flight as a student flyer, Ben's stomach turned over when the Wright dropped out from under them and left three inches of daylight between him and the plywood seat. Fos had jammed the elevator control forward and dived them beneath a circling buzzard with no more than ten feet to spare!

"I'd just as soon be strapped down," Ben said later as they lined up at the cook tent with the carnival roustabouts.

"Not while I'm head flyer. You never seen a crash. Hope to God you never do. Worse thing that can happen is fire or the engine falling on you. A strap'd just keep you in there to be roasted or mashed flat, Ben."

They patched fabric and tightened wires and flew more

practice flights and were tolerated by the roustabouts or razorbacks, as Rathrock called the tough laborers who did the heavy work and were at the bottom of the carnival's social standing. The slicksters who worked the midway and the sideshow people weren't so friendly, but the human cannonball, the Mighty Cordova, talked with them almost as equals.

He was a compact dark fellow with a pointed face and a moustache like an inked line across his upper lip. He hated the carnival food. "Cabbage! All the time cabbage. I am not a Russian peasant. Cabbage give me gas. If I swell up in the cannon, then we have some *grande* gun jam, no?"

At first, they had thought he was Italian. "No, no, *señores*! What do I want with spaghetti? *Arroz con pollo, enchiladas, chili con cordero.* Even a taco! In Mexico, real food! Here, cabbage. *Repugnante!* Ay, Max," he said to his sun-browned little assistant hunched on the bench beside him, "one day we find a town with real food, *sí*?"

"Cordova and Max are okay, but the rest of them don't exactly welcome us because they're worrying over the kind of competition we'll give them," Ben suggested.

"Them midway people?" Fos said. "They ought to like us fine. We're supposed to bring in more folks fer them to gyp."

"Bells afire!" Murf hooted. "Way you gallop all over the sky like a wounded pelican, Ben, who'd worry 'bout competition?"

The carnival finished its run at Claxton and creaked to Plainville. Ben made two more practice flights there. Then, on a pretty summer day suddenly gone chilly, Fos let the Wright rumble to a stop, jumped to the ground and shouted over the engine's idling clack, "You don't need me anymore, Ben. Take her up alone, try some turns, bring her back in as sweet as you just done."

Earlier this morning, he and Fos had flown around the nearly deserted carnival grounds outside Plainville. Fos rode in the passenger seat and Ben took the controls for his fifth flight as a student flyer. They bounced off the wet grass and circled the fairgrounds where Lucien Rathrock had set up his carnival. From five hundred feet, the midway and its brightly canopied stalls looked as pleasant as a county fair. But at night, Ben knew it would be the now-familiar kerosene-lighted strip of questionable games and outright gyps. In the sunlight, the sideshow tent was almost pretty from five hundred feet above, but Ben hated its close-up moldy grayness. The only new piece of equipment in Rathrock's Carnival Cavalcade was the big red chain-drive Mack truck. And it wasn't his. Specially outfitted as a platform for the giant silver cannon, its ugly snout sticking way out past the rear axle, the shiny rig belonged to the Mighty Cordova.

Now Ben pressed his feet against the crossbar to steady his wobbly legs and adjusted the borrowed goggles. Just off the left wing, Fos and Murf looked at the sky, the grass, anywhere but at him. Behind them, in front of the ragged sideshow tent, the carnival people had appeared like jackals. They seemed to have an instinct for this kind of thing. In their moth-eaten hides, Ben realized, they felt disaster coming.

He tore his eyes away from them and squinted down the lumpy field. This was why he had come here, wasn't it? This was really why he'd left Indiana and Horner's blacksmithy. Even if it meant being scared to death, he knew now that he'd come here not to be a mechanic's errand boy, but to fly. He took a deep breath of scorched oil fumes and fed in the raw gas.

The engine choked, backfired, then the big twin propellers kicked up grass and the Wright rolled forward.

Don't pull her off. Let her fly off. Give her a chance to build up steam . . . He could almost hear Fos's words over the engine racket.

The wings bit and held smoothly. The ground fell away. He had done it! He was up here alone! He had coaxed the aeroplane free of the ground and now pressed the thick warping lever to guide the machine through a glorious sweeping turn. He saw them all standing down there, shading their eyes, looking up, but not even dreaming of the incredible change that had taken place in him. He was a flyer!

In the next turn, a wind gust caught the high wings. He corrected without thinking, corrected beautifully. Did you see that, Fos?

In that moment, the old aeroplane had stopped flying him. Now he knew that he could make the Wright do whatever he asked of it. Flying was simple, after all! Five minutes ago, he had been a fumbling learner. Now he was certain he had mastered the air. Pepperidge. Beachey. Now Horner! Fos would know. Fos would understand that he couldn't put any of this into words that would make sense to anybody but another flyer. Fos would understand because they both were flyers now.

He cut back the power and set the Wright in a flat glide, a long sinking curve around the carnival's tents and stalls. The machine lowered evenly. He inched back the elevator lever. The double wheels brushed the stubble. He glued her on the skids with full-back lever. The aeroplane trundled to a stop without a bounce.

He switched off the engine, lifted his goggles and stepped down professionally. The reaction was amazing. His knees buckled and he grabbed a skid brace. His vision blurred and he turned to wipe his eyes quickly.

Murf trotted toward him and slapped his back. Fos stood

off a few feet, his hands in the pockets of his riding breeches.

"You might have taxied back to the end of the field where we tie her down," he said. "Now we gotta start her up all over again." But his voice held a smile, and Ben realized that was the way one flyer told another that now he was one of the breed.

They didn't talk about his solo flight all the rest of the day. He had worked a miracle, but once the congratulations were given, Fos and Murf had gone back to patching the Wright's thin fabric and adjusting her wires. A snappy breeze had sprung up in the early afternoon and had canceled any flying for the crowd. Ben walked down the midway, but the pitchmen and the crowds seemed to view him as just another carnival hanger-on in rumpled trousers, an oil-stained shirt, and a crumpled brown cap.

When they bedded down that night in the mildewed tent Rathrock had loaned them, Ben couldn't hold back any longer. "It was so easy!" he said in the darkness.

"Go to sleep," Fos muttered.

"But it *was* easy. There's just not all that much to it."

After a pause, Fos's voice cut like whip leather. "Easy! That's maybe what killed Hoxsey and Ely and Kelly and Oxley and Moisant and all them others. Maybe they thought it was easy, too. It is—when everything goes right. But you'll see how different things get when everything goes wrong. And it goes wrong in a finger snap. The wind stops holding you up and you got only dead weight under you. The grass ain't soft when you hit it going seventy. Don't say it's easy, Ben. You just ain't seen it when things go wrong."

Ben felt his face burn, and he was glad Murf had already doused the lantern. Fos wasn't what Ben had thought at all. Conqueror of the Clouds! That was a laugh. Why, the old man had no more nerve than a Sunday afternoon sports flyer. He didn't deserve to be billed as a flyer even with Rathrock's worn-out Carnival Cavalcade!

I'm the one with the nerve, Ben realized. He cradled his head in his hands and stared up into the darkness. If I work it carefully . . . work it right, the Conqueror of the Clouds can be, and in just a matter of weeks, Ben Horner!

7

In the two weeks they had been part of the carnival, Fos had flown only seven "shows." And those had been something short of sensational, nothing much more than wobbling back and forth across the grounds after a standard takeoff, dipping the wings cautiously, switching the tail back and forth. Ben was panting to get into the act.

Lucien Rathrock was panting right along with him. "Saw you take the machine up alone yesterday, Horner," he told Ben. "You able to put some juice in that flying act? Pepperidge don't exactly pack 'em in, and the Mexican cannonball only shoots on Sundays when his stomach feels right."

"It rained last weekend. That's what kept the crowd down."

"Last weekend, but not the one before that."

"We were just getting started then," Ben pointed out. "You can't expect a big act right off the bat."

Rathrock's weak eye fluttered hard in the morning sun. "When I hire a cooch dancer, she gets the yokels to pay those extra sideshow quarters the first time I put her in the back tent. When I take on a new wheelman, he starts paying off the first night he works a game on my midway. Cordova wowed 'em in Terre Haute, first Sunday he was with me."

"Before the cabbage got him."

"I'm not funning, boy. You stand here telling me two weeks isn't long enough for a warm-up. Other people I hire, I wouldn't put up with fooling around like you people do."

"We're not on your payroll, Rathrock."

"You're living off me. Tent's mine. Grub's mine." He stormed off toward the picket line of workhorses, then turned back. "It's Saturday again, Horner. Another chance to build a crowd. It'll be different this time."

"We'll try to make it different."

"I mean *I'm* making it different. Big chance—last chance. Can't afford to keep feeding you gents with nothing to show for it. You pull in a crowd this afternoon or pull out of here tomorrow."

Ben stuck his hands in his pockets and leaned back against a water wagon. These weeks had put muscles on him, had sharpened him. He was a flyer now, with a flyer's confidence. "No good," he said.

Rathrock reddened angrily. "What do you mean, no good?"

"If we put on a hot show this afternoon, it won't draw a

crowd out here until tomorrow, when the word gets around Plainville."

The carnival operator thought that over. "Yeah, you got a point. All right, you people put on a real show today, we'll check the gross tomorrow. That means from now on, that aeroplane's got to make hair stand up around here."

Ben felt a hand on his shoulder as Rathrock marched off. "Heard that last part," Murf said. "Bells afire, Ben, I can't blame him. We promised to pull in bigger crowds, but they just won't come out to see Fos fly back and forth a couple hundred feet over their heads."

"If he could just get himself to pull off something like he did in Hughesville, Murf."

"That made him worse, bouncing off the ground behind them sycamores. Oh, he didn't tell you 'bout that, did he? Yep, he smacked the ground when he pulled outta that dive. Split the left front skid. I fixed it in the dark that night. He didn't want you to know. Thought you'd figure he was slipping bad. He is, Ben, but try not to sour on him because of it. He was one good racing driver."

"Murf, the only thing I worried about is the kind of show we put on."

"I'll tell Fos when he gets back."

"Gets back? From where?"

"Plainville. Went off just after breakfast in one of the light wagons with Epps, the carnival doc. Said he just had to get away from things for awhile."

"That's just peachy," Ben said. "That seedy old horse doc is the worst possible kind of friend for Fos to take into town. You know and I know they've gone straight for the first barroom they spot." He hoped he sounded angry, but he was having a hard time hiding his excitement. With the old man mumbly drunk in Plainville, Ben himself could fly the act!

By two thirty, Fos hadn't returned. Rathrock was getting itchy. "That aeroplane's going to be in the air by four, or you freeloaders'll be out of here by five!"

At three, a rim of clouds puffed above the flat western horizon. Still no Fos.

" 'Fraid we both know what's happened," Murf said to Ben in the shade of a baseball-throw booth.

"Why would Fos do this on the day we need him most?" What he had to do, Ben realized, was maneuver Murf into asking him to make the flight.

Murf ran a blunt finger along a tent rope. "Because now you know how to fly the machine, too. Can't you figger it? The one thing that put him above both of us was that he was the only one who could fly the thing. Now that's gone. He's 'fraid of the kind of flying he has to do here. And I think he's a little 'fraid of you, Ben."

On the other side of the blue-striped tent wall, three hard-thrown baseballs slammed into the pyramid of wooden milk bottles. "It's a gyp!" a youthful voice howled. "I hit 'em fair and square."

The voice was right. Ben had learned that the six wooden bottles had been drilled and filled with chunks of iron bar, which made them next to impossible to clear off the wide ledge in the rear of the booth.

There were other refinements on the midway. The wooden hoops of the ring-toss game had just a paper-width of clearance over the cubes on which the prizes rested, and the rule was that a winning ring must encircle the cube as well as the cheap prize. The sights on the small rifles of the shooting gallery were set high and off center. A palmed magnetic weight could be clapped on the backs of the wheels-of-chance opposite numbers on which no customer had laid his nickel. Rathrock's carnival was a ragtag collection of concessions and crowd-producing acts, most of which were proof that the buyer must indeed beware.

The baseballs resumed their thud into the weighted bottles, and Ben scoffed, "Your theory's all wet, Murf. Fos afraid of me? That's ridiculous!"

"He ain't here, is he? And he won't be until he figures Rathrock's fired us. Then he'll come back and tell us we tried hard and failed, and him and me are going back to what we were doing before."

"You were starving before."

"But it was the kind of flying Fos could do. And he was getting whatever kind of glory went with it."

Ben's mouth tightened. "And now he's in Plainville with a bottle. We need a flyer or Rathrock's going to dump us."

"You're right. And you know what that means? There's only one other flyer I know of."

Good old Murf! Ben was elated, but he played out the game. "*Me?* I've got only fifteen minutes of flying alone! Lord, Murf, I could smash up the machine and kill myself in the bargain."

"Isn't that what they come to see?"

Ben stared at him, then laughed. "You're as cold-blooded as Rathrock. I could just forget this whole stupid business and walk out of here, you know. I don't owe anybody anything."

" 'Cept maybe to Fos for teaching you how to fly."

Ben let that go by. "I ought to wait until I've had more practice," he said, knowing that Murf wouldn't dare agree.

"The crowd'll never know."

"Barnum had nothing on you!" Ben squinted westward. The growing cloud masses covered a third of the sky, ballooning higher, iron gray at their bases. A chilly breeze ripped the grass.

Lucien Rathrock puffed around a lemonade stand, his head pivoting up and down the midway. "Where in tarnation is Pepperidge? He's got a show scheduled in ten minutes!"

"There'll be a show," Ben said, glorying in every word. "I'm flying it."

The carnival owner stood winking at them, then his face cracked into a hard little smile. "That, my boy, I will even watch myself."

The crowd had somehow gotten word of the coming drama—maybe even disaster, which would be all the more exciting, something to talk about around the warm Plainville stoves next winter. They lined the narrow flying strip, pressing forward to the cropped grass itself, until Rathrock sent out a crew of roustabouts to set up a rope-and-human fence.

The Wright poised at the end of the field, its twin pusher propellers swishing in the darkening afternoon. Beyond the empty passenger seat, the engine blipped and popped as smoothly as Ben could expect.

Murf stepped between the skids and thrust his face close. "You sure you remember how to fly this thing?"

Ben threw him a grin. "Who ever asks a sideshow flyer a thing like that?"

"Yeah." Murf reached back over the wing to make a final engine adjustment, then stood clear. Ben pulled up his goggles and tugged his backward cap lower. His feet jittered in excitement on the rudder bar. He moved the engine control, and the Wright rolled forward.

His takeoff wasn't as good as yesterday's, but he knew it didn't matter. Not to the crowd. They wanted to be thrilled, to feel their scalps prickle, to burst the tight-throated "Ahhh . . . !" from their lungs. The smoothness of his flying mattered not at all. They would appreciate only its recklessness.

The wings found their bite and the wheels bounced free. He climbed in a gentle turn that brought him back over the carnival. The air was clear but, to the west, clouds were still building. Lightning flickered behind their dark rolls. He knew he had to get his act over with in a hurry and put the machine back on the ground before the storm hit.

Abruptly he cut the power. The engine banged like a shotgun. The Wright plunged, its wires picking up the first keening of the wind wail that would tell the gapers below that the aeroplane was diving, perhaps, they would hope, out of control.

The tents grew larger, tilting as he banked to line up his dive along the flying field. The crowd strained forward, bulging the ropes the roustabouts struggled to hold against the surging shirtwaists and denim-clad bellies. They wanted to be scared? Fos had managed to do it a couple of times, though he'd been half scared to death himself. Ben could easily top that.

He tightened his grip on the thick rudder lever. The machine slewed to the left, skidding toward the crowd. He straightened the yawing aeroplane and lined up on the wavering line of roustabouts. The Wright sank lower, howled across the end of the field. He fed it power.

The crowd fell back on itself. Ben shoved the elevator control lever forward and back, zooming past the white-faced spectators not twenty feet off his right wings. The sense of power he'd felt when he'd first flown alone returned in a rush. He pulled into a steep climb toward the cloud mass spreading high above Plainville and turned to peer down through the open spars and struts of the tail planes. The carnival grew smaller below him, the crowd just a little clutch of white and yellow and pink dresses among the darker blotches of overalls and Saturday suits; a handful of confetti among toy tents beneath the huge sky.

The beating of the wind against his face slackened. Then the Wright shuddered and pitched forward, nearly tossing him from his seat. The engine picked up an unfamiliar beat. A warning flashed into his mind, a threat Fos had shouted in his ear over Claxton early one morning: *Let her go up too steep for too long, and she'll drop right out from under you!*

She sure had. He yanked the floppy elevator lever full back against its stop. But the machine fell even more steeply. The horizon rose over his head. He stared straight down into the green sea of an immense cornfield, feathery from this height, but it would be solid rock when he plunged through the leaves into the ground beneath.

Fos, why didn't you teach me more! Teach me how to get out of this hopeless dive that defies all rules of control. Nose down, lever back. The lever *was* back, but it might as well not have been there at all.

The engine was tearing itself to death. He cut back its howl. The shriek of wind through the rigging was louder than he'd ever heard it before.

Yet he must refuse to give in to the urge to throw his hands over his face and squirm upward from the impact. Fos had said that, too: *Fly all the way. Try anything. Just don't give up.*

Nose down, lever back. The rule didn't work. All right, if it didn't, try something else! He forced his clamped arm to move the lever forward. To his amazement, the screaming plunge slackened to a flatter dive. Tension returned to the control cables.

But the cornfield was too close. He had waited too long. *Fly all the way . . .* I will, Fos. All the way in. I'll still be trying when I hit.

The corn expanded to individual stalks. Tassels and leaves exploded over him in a tearing wave. He cringed against the final impact. But his hands stayed on the controls, working with an instinct he didn't yet know he had. The corn fell away. The Wright broke free. They staggered into clear air and climbed shakily. He throttled in more gasoline.

Elation dissolved the fear that had gripped him seconds before. He wouldn't feel the fear again until much later, on the ground, when sudden recall would send icy sweat running down his sides. But now, at five hundred feet over the Plainville fairgrounds, he laughed out loud in victory over the mysterious forces of the air.

It had been a stall, pure and simple. Climb too steeply, and the air over the wings was no longer smooth, but broken into whirls and eddies than wouldn't support the wings. The aeroplane became dead weight until the wings were brought back to the proper angle. For that, the elevator control went *forward,* not back. He had conquered the stall and his own stupidity. He was far more of a flyer than he had been moments before.

He circled the carnival. The air was no longer smooth. It was a washboard of bumps and jolts. The western clouds had built into a massive fortress that towered above him, flattening into an anvil of white against blue, dizzying miles above the Wright. The thunderstorm had moved too close while he fought the stall and survived the plunge to earth. Everything can go wrong in a finger snap, Fos had warned. Now the air tore at the frail aeroplane, tossed the wings high, then dropped it with a jolt that strained the fittings.

He bore in on the landing field, full power against the rising gale. His speed over the ground, thirty feet beneath the bucking wings, was little more than a fast walk. The great cloud wall was only two miles distant, rolling in hard. The brush line that marked the downwind end of the flying field crawled toward him, not nearly fast enough.

Half a mile ahead, the crowd had broken past the line of roustabouts and scattered all over the landing area. No matter. With the headwind holding him back, he would roll only a few feet along the grass—if he got there at all.

The storm thudded closer, black as oil smoke. Lightning flashed deep in its folds. He saw the misty rain line sweep forward along its base. The Wright bounced through a wild updraft. He fought it back down. The edge of the field danced closer, and the aeroplane reached for it.

Then an astounding change took place. The wind seemed to fade. The machine leaped forward, gaining speed even as Ben chopped power. A giant force thrust from the rear. The field rushed past in a horizontal waterfall of green.

The wind had shifted, shoving the biplane ahead like a chip riding heavy surf. Ben stuck the nose down. The skids struck the ground, threw a spray of dirt over him, and the aeroplane bounced hard. He felt the skid butts slap the turf behind him. The front of the machine dropped again and its wheels smacked down. He was rolling fast. The crowd scattered right and left, throwing each other aside to escape the onrushing aeroplane. He knew the terror they felt. He had done the same thing when Fos had dived on him near Hughesville.

But here there were too many people. He was going to plow straight through them, a horror the survivors would talk about far longer that next winter. He and they would be haunted by the disaster for the rest of their lives.

Fly it all the way. He did have some control left, not enough to get back off the ground and bounce over them, but enough, perhaps, to swerve sharply. It was a dangerous last-ditch thing to do, but failing to try it would be murder.

He clamped the rudder lever full back. The tail swung to the left, raced around him in a shower of dirt and grass clods. The machine canted heavily to the outside of the swerve. Then the lower wing caught the ground and swung the Wright fiercely in the opposite direction.

The suddenly reversed forces tore Ben from his seat. He was flung beneath the skid bracing wires and hit the ground hard. The left skid punched his shoulder as he rolled clear.

A cluster of hands pulled him to his feet. Murf's face broke through the tight circle. "You all right, Ben? You all right?"

A blast of wind spattered the first fat drops in their faces.

"Stakes!" Ben shouted. "Stakes and ropes. Fast!"

They pinned the Wright tight against the ground where she stood. There was no time to move her back to the work tent; just a few moments to pound in the stakes with big carnival mauls, then lash the wings and tail against the storm, which exploded over them in great sheets.

They ran for cover, and Ben sat shivering in the hangar tent on an upended gasoline tin while the wind tore at the canvas and shook the tent poles. He hadn't gotten a single cheer or clap or anything at all for his performance. The crowd had just melted into the storm.

The tent flap was thrust aside and Rathrock stuck his head in. Beneath his yellow oilskin whaler's hat, his face was soaked. "Not a bad try, Horner. But next time you use that diving-into-the-corn trick, how's about doing it closer to the crowd?"

His glance swept over Ben and Murf. "Storm's killed off things for a bit. Cook tent'll be open early. You figure out a decent show for tomorrow. Looks like you'll be with us for a while."

"Bells afire, you done it!" Murf cried as Rathrock ducked out into the rain. "You put us back in business, Ben. Wait'll Fos hears about this!"

Their eyes met, and Ben knew that now Murf, too, realized what really had happened today. They didn't need Fos anymore. They needed only the machine. Ben had schemed to make it come out this way, but he hadn't dreamed that it could happen so quickly.

8

The ponderous tackle wagon eased down the flatcar loading ramp, the roustabouts struggling against its weight, two of them on the high seat with their boots hard against the brake levers.

"Hold her. Hold her!"

A freight-yard worker wandered in close, and a carny man yelled, "Get back! She's liable to—"

Two of the men straining against the wagon tongue slipped on the dew-wet planks. Their feet whipped out from under them, and they sprawled among the legs of the unloading crew. The wagon's front wheels angled left, the big rig skidded sideways a few inches. Just enough. The left rear wheel dropped off the edge of the ramp. The clumsy tackle wagon collapsed off the gangway onto its side, its two brakemen flying into the rail-side weeds. The crash jarred the still-dark rail yard.

"God Almighty!" one of the roustabouts cried into the horrified silence. "It fell on him!"

The yard worker's scream knifed right down Ben's back. "Got him across the legs," he said in a choked voice.

"Come on," Murf yelled. "We'll give 'em a hand!"

He loped along the Parkton passenger platform. Ben raced after him. They bounded down the steps, across the tracks—and straight into Lucien Rathrock. He blocked their path like a crossing guard, his arms spread out.

"No need, no need. We'll take care of it. Get on out to the fairgrounds. Get your hangar tent set up. Go on, get out of here."

They retreated slowly, looking back as Rathrock began to direct rescue operations. "He's afraid that kind of thing'll spook us," Murf said. "Might at that. Wish we'd gone straight out to the fairgrounds in the first place, 'cept the Wright needs that gas."

After they'd managed to buy some tractor gas from an early-rising farmer, they had pulled into town just as the train arrived. Now they regretted the few minutes they had spent to watch the complicated process of unloading the carnival wagons from the flatcars.

The lizzie was parked on the other side of the Parkton station. Murf climbed in and set the throttle and spark levers. "Go ahead, Ben, turn it over." Ben grasped the crank and yanked. The auto coughed into life, and he scrambled aboard.

The gears rasped, and Murf guided the battered Ford

through Parkton's still-dark streets to the only road leading out of town to the north. The four cans of gasoline burped and gurgled on the floor behind the front seats. With the lizzie's top down, the morning air was cold against their faces. Ben shivered and turned up his jacket collar, but the chill hadn't come from the cold alone. He could still see the railroader's feet sticking out from under the toppled tackle wagon.

"That was the third accident," Murf said, as if he'd read Ben's thoughts. "The third accident."

"If you believe that accidents come in threes, then that should be the end of it."

"There's some of them carnival folks beginning to believe that Rathrock's running a jinx outfit. Mebbe I'm even beginning to think a little that way, myself."

Ben glanced at Murf's craggy profile, silhouetted against the gray sky. To the east, the horizon had begun to brighten, but it would be a while before the sun brought its warmth to these northern Missouri rangelands. The chain of accidents was upsetting, Ben had to agree. In late July, one of the youngest roustabouts had gotten in the way of a stake maul on the edge of Vandalia. He was carted into town with a crushed shoulder, and Rathrock left him there when they moved on. Not a week later, in Oxdale, a half dozen stakes anchoring the sideshow tent had pulled loose in a wind squall. The sagging canvas had swept one of the stocky "Little Egypt" dancers off her platform, neatly snapping her ankle. And now this morning, the rail-yard worker's legs had obviously been crushed beneath the tackle wagon on the Parkton siding.

"Jinx outfit," Murf repeated.

"Careless outfit," Ben countered, "but they'd rather believe it's a jinx. That's how those carnival people think."

Murf peered over the top of the windscreen at the rapidly

brightening sky. "It's clearing off. Guess Fos'll find us easily enough if that old bucket'll fly seventy miles."

Ben kept his eyes on the dirt road. "How do you think Fos will take it?"

"Take what?"

"The accident at the freight yard."

"Like he took the other two."

"He's as bad as Rathrock's people."

Murf snorted. "We're *all* Rathrock's people! Look at us, Ben. Ain't had a chance to wash my coveralls in two weeks. You look like you been rolled up in a laundry bag."

"I don't mean it like that. Fos tries to hide it, but I think he's as superstitious as the rest of them. He wouldn't fly the day the dancer was hurt. I flew that day, and saved us again."

"He was sick."

"Not in the morning," Ben pointed out.

"Well, he got sick in the afternoon."

"*After* the accident. He's getting worse, Murf. Off somewhere with a bottle half the time. Scared to put on anything but a fake flying show the other half."

Murf's face twisted. "Don't blame him too much, Ben. It's hit him hard that you can fly good's he can. Maybe better, far as Rathrock sees it. Them dips and sways Fos does don't fool everybody. Rathrock knows that the only time the crowd really comes to life is when you're up there. But Fos's way or your way, one of you is gonna kill hisself in that old windmill—Fos with his bottle or you with no brains."

The lizzie rattled across the loose planking of a bridge.

"Is that how I look to you, Murf?"

"Aw, Ben, what we're doing now is worse'n gypsy flying."

"But this is only the beginning," Ben protested. "Think

87

of what we've done already. You and Fos were going no place trying to carry passengers. Now we're flying for a circus." . . .

Ain't a circus. A carnival. A two-bit, second-rate carnival."

"All right, Murf. But it's a start. From here, we can go right on up into the big air meets."

"Don't rightly see how."

"You'll see soon enough. You stick with me, you'll see how." Ben would never admit to it, but Fos was playing right into his hands. Every time the old flyer was too far into the bottle, Ben flew the show. And Ben knew he was better at it. It was just a matter of time until the old man quit trying to fool them—and himself—and dropped out of the act altogether.

In the morning sun, Parkton's fairgrounds was a large sun-baked field three miles north of town, riddled with gopher holes and bounded by the dirt roadway from town on one side, a row of scraggly trees along the opposite boundary, and wire fences at each end. In the south section was a small dirt trotting track and four tiers of bleachers with flaking whitewash.

Two hours after the wagons had creaked out of the dust cloud that had drifted along with them in the still heat, Rathrock's shabby Carnival Cavalcade was set up and ready for whatever early business might straggle out from town. Nothing was going right. To begin with, the timing was all off. Setting up on a Sunday was the last way to make a buck. The idea was to set up on Friday, then cash in through the weekend. But the chartered locomotive that hauled Rathrock's six specially outfitted flatcars had burned out a bearing. That had fixed things just fine. They were more than two days behind schedule.

As if that weren't bad enough, around noon rumors of a rapidly growing disagreement spread the length of the midway and even to the sideshow area, where Ed Nolan, the "human skeleton," had one of his coughing fits while he was trying to tell the story. The chunky snake charmer was interested, but she kept on dribbling scarce water on the burlap she had draped over her two python cages. Ben had seen her struggling from the water wagon with a brimming-full fire pail, and she had gladly accepted his help.

"It's Cordova," Ed Nolan choked out. Ben and Murf had decided some time ago that the sickly human skeleton was in the final stages of consumption. By now, they had enough show-business fatalism to accept the fact that if Nolan wanted to die on the road, that was his business.

"Cordova," Nolan gasped, bending into another volley of coughs while Ben edged clear. "He won't shoot today."

Bess Kidwell—Ben had been surprised to discover that the circus people had ordinary names, then was surprised at his surprise—straightened up from her cages, set the pail aside, and slapped her hands on her huge hips. "Why won't he shoot? It's Sunday, ain't it?"

"Says he's sick."

"Cripes, Nolan, he's no sicker than y—— Cripes, Nolan," she began again, "we're all sick more'n half the time in this outfit." She poked a thumb at Ben. "Even these aeroplane drivers ain't too healthy. Their boss, anyways. I hope Rathrock *makes* Cordova shoot. How else we gonna get a crowd out here? I didn't see no broadsheets at all when we come through town."

"Getting toward the end of the season, Bess. Advertising money's all been spent. You know how Rathrock gets at the end of the season. Anything to bring in a buck except putting out a buck. He's got an iron thumb right on Washington's eyeball."

"Yeah, I know all right. He gets right desperate near season's end. Wanted me to use a rattlesnake last year, along with my babies. Pythons and boas ain't gonna hurt nobody if they're handled right, I told him. 'That's why you need a rattlesnake,' he says. 'You keep it from coiling up, it can't bite. That's how the Indians get away with dancing with 'em.' Well, he was right about that, but getting it in and out of the box would've been bad enough. I told him he would've sold tickets to that, too."

Bess Kidwell slapped Nolan's arm in glee. "Know what he says then? 'De-fang it.' De-fang it! They shed their fangs and grow new ones all by themselves. I sure told him what he could do with his rattlesnake."

Nolan choked and gasped out, "He could've sold . . . tickets to *that,* for sure!" He got control of himself and added, "Rathrock ain't asking Cordova to put a real shell in that cannon. He just wants him to do his reg'lar act at the reg'lar time."

The Wright clattered out of the east just after midday, circled the fairground noisily, then put down in the open north end, kicking up a dust cloud as Fos gunned it to the half-set-up hangar tent. He cut the switch and slapped at his coveralls. "Ever see so many gopher holes in one place? Thought I'd shake into a streak of sawdust and sweat on the landing roll."

He pulled his goggles down around his neck, climbed out of his seat, and ducked through the skid braces. " 'Nother twenny miles and I'd've fell outta the sky with a dry engine. Had to stop near Clay City fer gas as it was. You made any 'rangement fer gas here?"

"Bought four cans of it just outside of town," Ben told him. "Cordova was going to sell us some from his truck, but he says he's low, too. I didn't push too hard. He's got troubles enough."

"What's got into Cordova?"

"Claims he's sick. Bess Kidwell says we're all half sick, or half of us are sick all the time, or something like that. You don't look so great yourself."

"I'll be all right once I see Doc Epps."

"I know what that means," Ben said. Behind Fos, Murf made shutting-up motions, but Ben was determined to plunge straight into it this time. He was tired of the cover-up, the pretense that Fos was entitled to a little nip now and then. Lately, it seemed almost that Fos was sober just a few hours between bottles.

If the old flyer had been an ordinary falling-down drunk, the situation would have been simpler. But Fos could give the appearance of being cold sober when he was practically blind. The clue was that out-of-focus stare into space above your head. He could actually fly in that shape, as long as luck held. So far, it had.

Fos said in a tone as hard as iron, "I'll be ready to fly the show after I've seen the doc."

"After you've climbed into a bottle," Ben challenged.

"G'wan, Fos," Murf said hastily. "Ben's been up too long. We ain't slept fer nearly twenty hours."

"I don't hafta take anything from you," Fos barked at Ben. He moved closer, bristling like an angry rooster.

Murf quickly edged between them. "You ain't got much time, Fos. Rathrock'll want a show this afternoon. You know, the Sunday Special."

They watched the old flyer trudge toward the veterinarian's tent, hands shoved in the pockets of his faded jodhpurs. "You know what's going to happen as soon as the doc tells him about the accident this morning," Ben said. "I wonder how many bottles old Epps got stored for him."

91

Murf's face crumpled. "You ought to ease up on him, Ben. Things are getting to him real bad."

"That's his fault, not mine."

"Is it? You think him and me would've gotten into this crazy carnival stuff on our own? Not on your tintype, Ben. Wasn't till you come along that we even thought of it. How many times I hafta tell you that?"

"How many times do I have to tell you that you were starving to death before I showed you how to make money? I *know* we're making money now because I've made over a hundred dollars so far on my cut alone."

"Yeah, we're making money. But look what it's costing Fos."

"I don't buy his hooch," Ben said. He gazed after Fos long after Murf had gone into the hangar tent. "I don't buy his hooch," he repeated to himself.

They had watched Cordova being shot out of the cannon before, but today Ben sensed something different in the knot of carny people clustered around the entrance. He stood away from them with folded arms. But he couldn't stop his fingers from drumming on his biceps, and he finally shoved his hands deep in his pockets.

I've got late-season jitters, Ben thought. Or maybe it's just curiosity to see whether Cordova was sick or faking. Word had gotten around, and it had the power to draw nearly everyone, rubes and carny people alike, from the midway and sideshow into the pole-and-canvas enclosure where the huge silver cannon gleamed on its scarlet truck.

A hand thrust against Ben's back. "*Perdón. Perdón,* Ben." Cordova, pasty-white under his leather helmet, pushed through the crush at the entrance to the high canvas arena.

"He does look sick," Ben told Murf. "I'll be back in a minute." He scrambled through the crowd and clapped a hand on Cordova's shoulder. "Hey, you all right?"

The Mexican cannonball turned in annoyance, then smiled faintly. "Ah, Ben. Look at me. Do I look right?" He shrugged. "I live up to my agreement. *Ay,* Max, *está usted listo?* Are you ready?"

From the rear deck of the big seat-over-engine chain-drive Mack, little Max whirled the elevating wheel. The muzzle of the giant gun inched upward.

The argument between Rathrock and Cordova had eaten up the afternoon. Because of wind and blowing dust, the flying show had been canceled, but now the air was dead still. To make up for the loss of his Sunday Special aeroplane show, it was obvious that Rathrock had purposely spread word of his problem with the human cannonball.

Around the inside perimeter of the enclosure, roustabouts had lighted the kerosene torches on their high poles. The upturned faces of the crowd were wide-eyed in the glare. Torch smoke spread above the enclosure in a thick layer.

Ben worked his way back to Fos and Murf. "He's not in such good shape, at that. Sick or scared, or both."

"Scared of what?" Murf asked. "He's done this fool act a hundred times."

"Scared of the jinx," Fos said. His lips were dry and cracking. He licked them quickly with a pale tongue. He had kept his word this afternoon, returning from Doc

Epps's tent just in time to learn that he didn't have to fly after all.

"Come on, Fos," Ben prodded. "You don't believe in jinxes."

"Dunno. Three accidents. Three people busted up. They say reg'lar accidents come in threes, but in jinxed outfits they go on and on."

Cordova had pulled on white gloves and was mounting the iron rungs set along the top of the steeply sloped barrel. "Ladies and gentlemen," Rathrock boomed through a battered fiberboard megaphone, "the Mighty Cordova, the Human Cannonball, is about to astound you with a feat of daring the likes of which you have never seen before! Fired from the muzzle of a giant cannon, hurled through empty space without protection of any kind but a leather helmet, the Mighty Cordova is about to defy death before your very eyes!"

They had heard this spiel every weekend since joining Rathrock's Cavalcade, but the buildup never failed to tighten Ben's stomach and send an uncomfortable ripple down his back. Even without Rathrock's overdone shouting, the shoot was quite a spectacle.

More people paid their four bits and pushed into the temporary arena. As the place filled, Ben, Fos, and Murf found themselves pushed forward until they stood at the edge of the space that the roustabouts kept open between the gun truck and the net.

Rathrock strutted beneath the uplifted gun muzzle. The shabbiness of his old boots, faded corduroy trousers, patched red shirt, and ancient cowboy hat were overlooked in the torch glare. He was the ringmaster now, and Ben sensed that this was Lucien Rathrock's single moment of glory in each week of squabbling sideshow freaks, shyster wheelmen, and crumbling equipment.

Rathrock tilted his megaphone to lift his hoarse baritone over the crowd. "Only seconds now . . . only seconds until the Mighty Cordova is propelled through one hundred feet of thin air by a massive explosive charge! If you are still outside, hurra, hurra, hurra! For the price of only one half dollar, you will see a spectacle so amazing that you'll tell your grandchildren about it, talk about it for decades to come. So hurra, hurra!"

Aloft on the huge muzzle, Cordova looked down into their faces. He seemed to stare right at Ben. Then he shrugged in a hopeless little gesture. At that moment, the sun's last glow broke through the low clouds on the western horizon and turned Cordova's white coveralls a brilliant orange. He appeared to pull himself together, saluted the crowd with an upraised arm, then lowered himself feet first into the cannon's mouth. His fingers held his head and shoulders above the rim for long seconds. Then he disappeared down the barrel.

The net at the far end of the big canvas ring was a tough mesh of quarter-inch rope. Fifteen feet wide and twenty feet high, it was supported by two heavy poles sunk into the ground and guyed on three sides. The net's bottom edge was pulled forward and staked down some fifteen feet from the two supporting poles, so that the net formed a taut sloped rectangle a hundred feet from the gun truck.

"The trick," Cordova had told them between the fits of temper that had kept him out of the big-time circuses, "is to pull the net tight enough so you won't stretch it to the ground when you hit. But it must be loose enough so it won't spring you back out. Then there is the—how you say—the roll-down after you hit. It must be done *con perfección*. No mistakes. No room for mistakes."

Rathrock's amplified voice boomed into the crowd, rising and falling as he swung the megaphone around the makeshift arena. "Now, ladies and gentlemen, the moment has come! The moment of fear. The moment for nerves of iron. If some of the ladies cannot stand such excruciating excitement, I advise them to turn their backs or cover their faces." The burly carnival owner strode to the edge of the crowd and turned his megaphone on Max at the control handle just behind the truck's cab. "Are you ready?"

"*Sí, señor!*" came the faint reply.

"On the count of five," Rathrock shouted, his bad eye blinking faster in the torchlight. "One . . . two . . . three . . ."

The crowd noise died. Beyond the canvas wall, Ben heard the distant cry of a peanut vendor. Then that, too, faded in the hot silence.

"Four . . ." Rathrock gave them a long, almost unbearable pause. Behind him, Ben heard a man's choked voice: "Great Lord Almighty!"

"FIVE!"

Max's arm swung down. A sharp *twang* was swallowed in a blast that shook the ground and deafened the crowd. The Mighty Cordova flew from the muzzle, white smoke bursting behind him. High over the center of the arena, body stiff, arms plastered to his sides, he arched through the torches' kerosene smoke, then hurtled toward the net. Cordova bent sharply forward at the last possible moment. He struck head down, the small of his back taking the impact.

He hit low and off center. A front retaining stake snapped. The lower right corner of the net flew inward. The slack netting closed around Cordova as he smacked the ground, kicking up dust.

A scream knifed the breath-held stillness. Then everyone ran for the crumpled net.

"Back, please!" Rathrock shouted. "Back, ladies and

gentlemen, for God's sake. Give us room. Little accident, that's all. Give us some room!"

Ben had to give him credit. Rathrock could keep his head. The roustabouts tore at the net tangle. "Easy, boys!" Rathrock called. "Don't bust him up any more than he is."

Ben pushed through the crush, Murf and Fos close behind him. "I hope the crowd got what they wanted," Ben said to Murf. "A real half-buck's worth."

"Hold it, boys," Rathrock said, blocking their way. "No use you getting into it. Razorbacks'll take care of everything." He scowled at Ben and Fos. "No good, you seeing something like this. It's got nothing to do with the flying act, you hear? Nothing at all."

"Tell that to Fos, not to me," Ben said as he shoved past.

Cordova was white as poster paste, his eyeballs rolling up into his head, his legs at bad angles. A roustabout grabbed him under the arms.

"Suavemente! Gently, *por favor!"* Max shouted as he burst past Ben, thrust the roustabout aside and bent over the crumpled human cannonball. *"Qué ha pasado, León?* What happened?" He turned to the crowd helplessly, tears streaming down his leathery cheeks.

"Come on, boys," Rathrock urged the clustered roustabouts, "get a board and slide him on it gentle-like, you hear me?" He pulled Max away without force. "They'll take care of him. You go get the gun truck stowed and help with the net." To Ben he said, "Poor little guy. Better to give him something to do than to let him look at that."

Three of the carny laborers got Cordova on a pine plank, tied him in place with canvas straps, and took him into town in the best-sprung wagon Rathrock had. A while later they creaked back into the fairgrounds without him. Ben watched them go into Rathrock's office wagon, its door opening a yellow panel in the night. They came out a few minutes later, and Ben asked as they walked past the hangar tent, "How is he?"

"Busted his neck, fella," one of the men said over his shoulder as if that happened every evening. "He's dead."

Ben went back into the tent and looked at Murf and Fos. His eyes stayed on Fos. The old flyer sat hunched up on a gas tin, a blanket over his shoulders, though the air was heavy. "You all right?"

Murf shook his head in a silent signal.

"T'tell the truth, I ain't worth the powder blown to pot, Ben," Fos admitted. His voice was a dry whisper. The red eyes wobbled up. "This whole stupid thing ain't worth a fritterin' damn. Knowed that 'fore Cordova got hisself bunged up. Nobody'd listen."

Ben looked at Murf quickly, then back at Fos. "Cordova's dead."

Fos brought his eyes back up to Ben's face with an effort that seemed to hurt him. "Gawd!"

Murf said, "But he didn't look—"

"Broke his neck."

From inside his blanket, Fos pulled a flat bottle. "No use foolin' any longer. Anybody want any of this? . . . I guess not." He upended the pint, and they could hear the hard swallows.

"Bells afire, Fos!"

"It's no use, Murf. I knowed that a long while back. I'm seeing snakes. One day I'll be up in that thing, and I'll see the snakes up there and then I'll be dead like Cordova." He wiped his mouth with the back of his hand. "Won't that be something? Trying to outfly a water moccasin a thousand feet up."

Murf got up from his bedroll, walked over to Ben, and said quietly, "He's been like this since Cordova's accident. I didn't think he was this bad."

"I guess he's been this bad for quite a while. Tonight just brought it into the open."

Fos took another noisy swig. "And scorpions. I seen them, too. They're worse'n snakes. Too small. Can't find 'em all. . . ."

"Fos," Murf pleaded, "ferget it. Go to bed."

"They got a little sting you barely feel, then your leg gets numb, then it creeps up, up into your head." He held the bottle neck down. "Anybody got any more?" His eyes came into focus briefly. He stared at them. "Naw. You two won't give me sweat. Jus' let me sit here an' die. Aw, Murf, it's never been the same since that Ben joined up with us. We had fun 'fore that, didn't we, Murf?"

He reached back to push himself to his feet, but he couldn't make it. "Hey, Murf. Hey, you 'member that time in Oneonta? 'Member that black-haired woman I took up over the fact'ry where she worked? She come close to killing me, wanting to fly the machine herself! 'Member that, Murf?"

"I remember, Fos."

"Ain't been the same since he joined up with us."

"We're making money, Fos."

"It's killing me. I'm scared, Murf. Scared all the time. One poop outta that engine, and it's me they'll tie to a plank. I don't wanna die, Murf. I don't. I jes' wanna have it be like it was before. If it can't be like it was, then le's sell the fritterin' machine an' le's go do something else."

His eyes suddenly glazed, and he tilted sideways off the gasoline tin. Murf caught him, laid him on a blanket, and folded it over him. Ben's throat worked. "I've never seen him like that!"

"Worst he's been. I swear, he's gonna kill hisself, we let him get up in the air many more times."

Ben wiped his palms down the sides of his trousers. Fos

100

was right, even if he was drunk. This couldn't go on. Not this way. The old man was dragging them all down with him. A flash of anger swept through Ben. "This does it! I'm going to see Rathrock."

The carnival owner, shirtless, was bent over his packing-crate desk at the far end of the cluttered lantern-lit business wagon. He squinted sideways at the doorway. "It's pretty late, boy."

"This can't wait."

Rathrock began to slide his chipped enameled cup behind an overloaded bill spike, then he noticed the frosted gin bottle was in full view. "Ah, well, you can't blame a man for taking a snort after a day like this one. You want any?"

Ben shook his head. "Sorry to hear about Cordova."

"We're all sorry. He was a nice-enough fella in his way." Sweat ran down the neck of Rathrock's grimy undershirt. The top two buttons of his trousers were open to ease his stomach roll. "What's on your mind?"

"I want an aeroplane of my own."

The cup stopped halfway to Rathrock's mouth. "That's wonderful, kid. I want a carnival of my own. A half dozen banks own this one."

"I'm serious."

"Aw, look, Ben. Is this anything to come in here with tonight? I don't need talk. I need this cup of gin and some sleep. The sheriff's been here, and there'll be papers to go over in the morning. Maybe reporters, too."

"The sheriff?"

Rathrock looked at him blankly. "Yeah . . . oh, I get you." He nodded at a stool. "Sit down. There was nothing out of line. Routine accident. The net anchor stake had a knot in it."

"That's routine?"

"I don't mean it that way. I mean it was an accident. This business has risks. You come in here to badger me; I don't need it." He took another drag from the cup.

Ben drummed his fingers on the edge of the camp stool's canvas. "Maybe I'd better start over. I'm afraid that unless . . ." He couldn't bring himself to say it. "I'll put it this way. If I had an aeroplane of my own, I could help you pay off those banks a lot faster than we're doing it now."

"Not a chance. One, what makes you think you'd do better if you owned the machine? Two, I don't want to be a partner in any aeroplane business. Three, where in God's dusty countryside do you think the money would come from?"

Ben tried to sound confident. "One, I'd like to try things Fos and Murf won't let me try now. Two, I came in to ask for a loan, not a partner. And three, I'll guarantee to make money for you—in spades."

"You got big ideas." Rathrock's voice softened. "Like me once. Just like me." He knocked back the last swallow in his cup and poured another two inches.

"Know what a mud show is, Ben? Used to be a hundred little circuses going from town to town by horse wagon on what passed for roads in those days. Mud most of the season. That's how the shows got their name. Came out of New York State just above the big city. 'Cradle of the Circus' they called it up there around Brewster and Danbury, Connecticut. P. T. Barnum, himself, was from Bethel, not fifteen miles away. I worked that lousy little mud show of mine out across the state, over the tip of Pennsylvania, then into Ohio. Couldn't make mor'n fifteen, twenty miles in one jump."

He shifted his bulk in his chair and gazed into the kerosene lantern, his bum eye weirdly blinking. "I got ideas about then. Like you. I got sick of grifting the rubes and rat-sheeting the big outfits. I wanted to go to Sunday school with a *real* circus, a big clean one with two, maybe even three rings. Steam calliope, aerialists, menagerie. The works. Twenty years later, after sticking my neck out a mile, I had one."

Smoke began to twist out of the lamp and Rathrock adjusted the wick wheel. "Ever hear of the Great Eastern and Western Circus? That was mine, in ninety-one. For just a year. We traveled in style that summer. By rail in thirty-four flatcars, special cars that used Bill Coup's piggyback system for loading and unloading. Yeah, I knew Coup. And the Ringling boys. Even met Yankee Robinson once, year before he died in the ring. That's the way I hope I go, Ben. Out there working the audience. Anyway, when we hit town—and we only hit the big ones then—by God, they knew we were something! I swear you could hear that steam calliope five miles. We'd parade our dozen elephants right down the main drag."

He leaned back in his creaky chair and clasped his hands behind his head. "The Great Eastern and Western Circus. It was something, Ben. I was going to be bigger'n Pogey O'Brien!"

"But with thirty-four cars and all, what—"

"What happened? First it was a fire in Toledo. Then some sickness hit the horses in Evansville. Lost most of them. But what finished us off was a Kansas flood. Can't even remember the name of the nearest town. Don't want to, I guess. The track was up four, maybe five feet above the prairie. Water stretched out for miles, no more'n six feet deep at the most. Then we hit a trestle. Long son of a gun, it was. I still remember how it shook under us just before it went."

"It collapsed?"

"Like a pile of matchwood. Lost all but six flatcars. All

the rest went down. Gone like that." Rathrock snapped his pudgy fingers.

"In just six feet of water?"

"That's what I thought until I saw the cars ahead of mine peel off the track behind the engine and just disappear, one after the other. That trestle was smack over the Arkansas River. In about the time it takes for a good sneeze, twenty-eight cars, all my animals, nineteen of my people were at the bottom of the Arkansas. Would have lost the whole train if a coupling hadn't broke. But the accident ruined me good. Only managed to salvage those six cars down there on the siding in Parkton. If you were to scrape off that orange Carnival Cavalcade paint, you'd find red and gold under it. Red and gold Great Eastern and Western Circus paint. That's all that's left, Ben. Now I got to put up with a bunch of sharks on the midway, freaks that got nowhere else to go, and whatever specials I can get my hands on. Tonight I lost the best I had."

Ben grasped the tops of the stool legs to quiet his drumming fingers. "That's what I'm here about. I think I can get Fos and Murf to sell me that aeroplane for a few hundred."

"I told you, I don't want to go into the flying business. I got enough problems with a human skeleton who's about at the end of his rope, and a ticket taker who claims one of my razorbacks is a thief, and a sideshow tent that's no more'n a network of patches."

"I'm talking about a loan," Ben interrupted, "but I'll earn the money back fast enough. The point is that I've got to get that aeroplane quick."

"You see it, too."

Ben was silent.

"Come on, boy, don't play games. I'm talking about the look Fos is wearing these days. Saw that look in the eyes of a wire walker once. Just before he missed a simple-enough step, and the razorbacks were scraping him out of the tanbark. How bad is Fos?"

"He's all right," Ben lied.

Rathrock grunted. "How far you willing to go to get that machine?"

"I'm not willing to steal like you do every day on the midway," Ben bristled. "I'm talking straight business."

"Calm down, Ben, calm down. What just came to mind is strictly legit. Takes nerve, but anybody'd go up in that squirrel cage you fly must have the kind of nerve I'm thinking about."

Ben's mouth went dry. "If I'm thinking what you're thinking . . ."

Rathrock leaned forward, eyes coming to life. "Look, it's not all that dangerous. Suppose I was to pull up stakes here. Town's no good anyway. And we get over to Mt. Olive near St. Louis—in one jump. Be set up by Friday. We'll bill you as . . . I got it! 'Suicide Horner'!"

"My God!"

"That's just to hook the rubes. You do the cannon act three times—"

"Three times!"

"Season's getting short, Ben. Gotta act fast. You do it next Friday, Saturday, and Sunday. I'll pay you enough to buy that aeroplane."

"You're out of your mind!"

"You want to get your hands on the machine before Fos smacks it up? You better act quick. I've seen a lot of performers fall apart in my day, and Fos looks like he's right on the edge." He tossed back another slug of gin. "Tell you what. You can have a practice try before—"

"The hell with practice!" Sweat had broken out on Ben's

forehead. "It has to be right every time. What's the sense of practice?"

"That's the way to talk. That *is* the way to talk!" Rathrock thrust the gin bottle at him. "Take a drag. But don't let me see you within a mile of the stuff before you climb into that cannon."

10

Ben was determined that he was going to win out. He bullied the shaky flyer, pushed in wherever Fos left an opening, threw in his face all the times they had waited for the old man to stumble back to the carnival, red-eyed and dragon-breathed. He backed Fos up against the fact that his nerve was gone, that he was actually costing them money now. It was brutal, unfeeling, but Ben told himself that he had to do it.

Murf sat on an empty gasoline tin, elbows on his knees, staring at the turf floor of the tent. His silence and uneasiness didn't stop Ben. He felt as sorry for Fos as Murf did, or so he told himself. But he didn't let up until the old flyer at last shouted, "All right, all right! You get the money together in one pile, you can have my part of the fritterin' aeroplane. I'm sick of it all! Sick of the rotten crowds, sick of you and Murf. Both of you!"

His voice broke. "I don't mean that, Murf. Machine's part yours. What about your half of it?"

"Whatever you decide, Fos."

"Take it, then!" the old flyer snapped at Ben. You get the money in one pile, you can have the fritterin' machine." He slapped the tent flap aside and tramped off into the darkness. Then his head popped back in. "If you get the money!"

They both gave Ben the silent treatment after that. The hangar tent was dismantled in silence, and during the ride to Mt. Olive, just west of St. Louis, Murf spoke only the minimum words necessary. Ten miles out of Mt. Olive, Fos clattered over their heads in the Wright, but he didn't waggle the wings or give any sign of greeting. He was waiting for them beneath the Wright's wings when they chugged into the fairgrounds. Chewing a cigar, he nodded at Murf but ignored Ben.

So what, Ben told himself. Either you did what you had to do and got somewhere, or you sat around being a nice fellow and the world went right past you.

In the mess tent at noon of the Friday he was to shoot, one of the Little Egypt dancers offered to launder his old coveralls. Cordova's flame-resistant suit had been too small for him. Max had suggested the coveralls Ben wore every flying day. "Even if you're dumb, you can be clean," she told him. She was much shorter than he, but probably just as heavy. Her voice was surprisingly soft, and she moved gracefully in spite of her weight.

She brought the coveralls back to him at four, grease

stains rubbed almost out, then carefully masked with chalk. It was the first kind move any of the regular carnies had made, and he didn't know what to make of it. The cloth smelled of powerful naphtha soap and was still damp. That might help, he thought, if there were sparks. He knew little of what went on in the huge barrel, even after Max's explanation, but he was sure it was frightening. Cordova had been the only one who really knew.

Darkness crept over the fairgrounds much too early for Ben. The crowd began to gather at the entrance to the cannon enclosure like vultures. Up on the bally platform, Rathrock harangued the crowd without letup, and he got most of their half dollars and had them jammed inside by eight fifteen. It was time, time to go through with it.

In the hangar tent, Ben pulled on the coveralls while Murf and Fos watched silently. Max had told him, "Tie the bottoms. And pray a leetle."

Max had told him more but not nearly enough. "Ees not so hard, maybe. Make the legs stiff. Arms down. Look up weeth the head . . . Boom! Then arms out straight. Then heet the net weeth the back end first."

"You ever done this yourself?" Ben had asked him.

Max stared into his grease can. "I am not Cordova."

"Neither am I."

"But you are too young to know eet," Max had said.

Buttoning the coveralls, Ben turned to leave the hangar tent. Suddenly Fos spoke. "Ben, you're crazier than a bent bird. You sure must want that aeroplane bad."

Ben looked at him, trying not to show the fear that had been building inside him since sunup. "It's as good as mine, Fos."

He pushed out of the tent, strode up the midway, pushed

through the crowd into the canvas-walled enclosure, and climbed onto the truck body. This had to be done fast, before his nerve wilted.

"There he is, folks!" Rathrock roared through his megaphone. "Suicide Horner, eager to defy death, to look into the very eyes of the Grim Reaper and say, 'Not this time!' " Rathrock's voice dropped for dramatic effect. "Or will this be the night that death takes no holiday? Will Suicide Horner's very first try at being a human cannonball also be his last? Remember, folks, he's never—I say, *never*—done this before."

He lowered the megaphone and wiped his mouth with his sleeve. He loves this, Ben realized.

"And now, ladies and gentlemen, Rathrock's Carnival Cavalcade gives you Blasting Benjamin Suicide HOR-NER!" He made frantic "up" motions to Ben.

Ben's legs were jelly. He had to drag them up behind him, and his calf muscles trembled all the way along the fat barrel. He placed each shoe carefully on the iron rungs already slippery from the sweat of his hands. He climbed past the level of the enclosure. Beyond the kerosene flares, he could see the glow of gaslights along the St. Louis streets a few miles eastward.

The muzzle was immense and slick with evening dew. Ben's hands shook on its thick lip. Could they see that from the ground? The frantically printed broadsheets Rathrock had plastered all over St. Louis had done their work. The crowd bulged the canvas enclosure, their upturned faces ruddy in the torchlight.

Rathrock's voice boomed through his ratty megaphone, but now the words were meaningless to Ben. Only the giant barrel had meaning. He had been surprised to find it made of wood, painted to look like steel and sheathed with metal only around the muzzle on the outside and some eight feet into the bore. Yet it looked lethal enough with its silver-enameled surface glinting in the flares.

He slid his hands downward to the far side of the muzzle opening and hoisted up his legs. It seemed obvious that his hips would jam, but he dropped down easily, his feet slipping along the sloped bore, feeling for the platform that was the top of the big spring-loaded piston. He had helped Max crank the spring down, and he knew its power.

Head just above the muzzle, he hung there, squinted down, and found them. Fos and Murf. Their faces showed . . . what? Disbelief, he decided. He hardly believed this himself. He twisted to look down along the barrel. At the control panel far below, Max nodded, but his face was expressionless.

Ben relaxed his grip and let the cannon's mouth rise past him. Before his shoes touched the piston head, he saw a scatter of the evening's first stars across the muzzle's gray disk. The back of Cordova's leather helmet rubbed against the paper-wrapped gunpowder squib packed in its slot two feet below the end of the barrel. The black powder would be fired by a trigger device when the piston tripped it at the end of its thrust.

He slid his arms down the metal sheathing and pressed his palms against his thighs. The barrel was hot. Sweat ran into his eyes, and his hair crawled with it beneath the white helmet. His stomach muscles had tightened so that he could barely breathe. He tensed his leg muscles and held his face out from the bore's surface. "Don't let the head bounce forward when I fire," Max had warned, "or zeep! No nose."

The wait was unbearable. Max, for Lord's sake . . . Then he remembered the signal they had agreed on. He kicked the barrel twice with sideways swings of his foot.

From far below, he heard Max's two answering raps on

the barrel. He counted silently. *One and two and three—*

His legs jammed into his pelvis. The giant barrel whooshed past him and fell away. A great orange flash spurted up a blast of heat. The black powder concussion slammed the soles of his shoes like a hard-swung board. The detonation left his ears singing.

He soared upward. The distant net was smaller than a handkerchief, slowly turning. He was tumbling. He threw his arms over his head and stiffened his legs. The net was bigger, rolling in from over his shoulder. Sky and ground chased each other around him. Wind tore into his mouth, ripped at the coveralls.

The net raced up to smash him full in the face. He flipped around like a frantic fish falling from a line and managed to hit the wire-hard roping sideways. His hip grated as the net rebounded and rolled him down and off in a flailing heap.

He stood up shaking. A fierce pain slashed through him, then the hip crunched back into place.

Murf was all over him, yelling, pounding his back like he'd made the winning touchdown in the last seconds of play. He looked past the wild-eyed mechanic. Just before the oncoming crowd swallowed Fos, Ben saw him turn away, shaking his head.

"Ain't worth the powder blown to pot!" Ben shouted at him hysterically. He'd never felt such a sense of incredible accomplishment. The mob surged around them. Ben and Murf had to shove their way out of the enclosure.

Fos disappeared. He didn't show up at the mess tent, and well past midnight, he still hadn't returned.

"Know'd he'd do this," Murf said, blowing out the kerosene lantern. "Know'd it the minute you got the cannon idea in your head."

"Don't blame me for Fos's problems."

"You sure changed things fer us, Ben. There's no mistake 'bout that. I ain't saying we wasn't heading fer trouble the way things were, but at least it was Fos's own trouble."

"It's still his trouble."

"But you've made it so's he can't live with it no more."

Ben didn't answer. He was tired of answering. Times changed, and if you didn't change with them, then you ended up like Fos and Murf, looking for the big break in a world that had already turned right past you.

By dawn, Ben's right side was an agonizing knot. Fos was still missing. Murf snored softly in his blanket on the far side of the Wright. Just as well, Ben thought through a wave of pain. He didn't want to talk to anybody.

He grabbed the Wright's tail-boom framing and hauled himself out of his tangled bedroll. He hadn't slept much and was glad daylight had come. He limped outside, bent over against the ache. Walking seemed to help, and he forced himself to keep moving. The carnival was waking up around him as he sat down in the mess tent with a groan.

"Here. I brought you some coffee." It was the Little Egypt dancer, her chunky face, narrow brown eyes, and broad mouth screwed into a touching grimace of concern.

"I ruined your wash job on the coveralls," he said.

"I'll do them over. Every day you do the stunt, I'll do them."

He looked up at her again. "What's your name?"

"Farah."

"Oh, come on. Your real name."

"Clara. Clara Dembrowski. Isn't that some name for an Egypt dancer?"

"You're good at it. Where'd you learn?"

She laughed. "Made it up. If you never saw real Egypt dancers before, I guess we look all right."

He finished the coffee, and she returned to the mess line for another, bringing a cup for herself, too. "Can I sit down?"

He studied her broad, high-cheeked face beneath its stacked mound of brown hair. She could never be pretty, even if she were to lose twenty pounds, but she had a plain, open look that was attractive. She was a lot more attractive, in fact, in her muslin work dress than in the tawdry dancing pantaloons and loose jacket.

"I'm from downstate Illinois," she offered. "Across the Wabash from Vincennes. You?"

"Indiana."

"Where in Indiana?"

"You know anything about Indiana?" His hip was murder, but he tried not to show it.

"Only Gary. I have an uncle there."

"I'm from Indianapolis."

"Why'd you leave?"

He really didn't want to talk, not at dawn to a fat girl from Illinois when his hip was killing him. "To get away," he muttered.

"From what?"

He looked up, touched by her earnestness. "To break out of what my family had planned for me. I'm no blacksmith."

"That's like me," Clara said. "I couldn't clean up after one more cow. So I just left there when the carnival came through last year."

"You like this better? All those rubes watching you up there, half dressed?"

She gave him a quick glance. "Does that bother you? I've

done it so many times, it doesn't mean a thing anymore. If that's what they want to pay for, I'll take the money. Finish your coffee and I'll go back with you and get your coveralls."

They caught Murf in his long underwear, and he tried to burrow back beneath the blanket. "Bells afire, Ben! Ought to know better'n bring a lady in here."

Ben ignored him, handed Clara the powder-stained coveralls, and she ducked back out of the tent. "That was no lady," he said to Murf, "that was an Egypt dancer."

Without Fos and with Ben barely able to walk, there would be no aeroplane show. Rathrock wasn't disturbed at the news. "You're pulling such a mob with the cannon, I don't need the aeroplane. Just don't kill yourself tonight, Ben. There's still a day to go."

Through the day, Ben worked with Murf on the Wright, his hip easing as the hours wore on. They stripped the engine and went over every part looking for hairline cracks or other warnings of troubles to come. "I don't know why I'm doing this," Murf grumbled. "Either this old banger is going to be yours come Monday, or Fos'll splatter hisself in it 'fore winter sets in."

"Pride of workmanship," Ben said. "What Murf Murfine touches runs like a clock."

" 'Cept this old crock. More like a stopwatch."

Neither of them mentioned Ben's coming shot that evening, but he knew they were both thinking about it. He could barely force down lunch. Cabbage. He thought of Cordova, pathetic little Cordova with his stomach trouble, his close bond with Max, then his sudden end in a loose net. Some way to try to make a living.

When the sun neared the flat Missouri horizon, Ben's throat went dry. His hands and feet seemed to move on their own, detached from his body. Was this how criminals felt while they waited for the hangman? Clara brought him the newly laundered coveralls, smiled quickly and said over her shoulder as she scurried away, "I hope you break a leg."

Ben was thunderstruck. "Why did she say *that*?"

"Heard tell it's some kind of show-business superstition," Murf said. "Actually s'posed to mean good luck."

At sundown, the torches flamed and a new crowd began to drift into the cannon enclosure. The barrel was an ugly silhouette against the sky, a stiff fat finger. Tonight was worse than last night because now he knew exactly what was going to happen. He knew the leg-crunching power of the piston, the searing flare and crash of the powder charge, the stunning impact of the net.

He walked quickly to the base of the giant gun, trying to swagger a bit but not knowing if he succeeded. He climbed numbly, lowered himself into the cannon's maw before he could change his mind. As his feet hit the piston, he realized he hadn't heard Rathrock's shouting nor seen the crowd's gape-jawed stare. He was in a living nightmare, noticing nothing but himself.

He kicked the side of the barrel and sucked in the pain in his side. The big plunger punched him into space. He got his arms out this time, just as the concussion slammed past him. He held himself straight, but he tumbled forward too soon. The net caught him full in the backside. His right leg popped through the roping. On the rebound, he hung head down, helpless in the wave of agony that gagged him.

"Give it up," Murf pleaded. "This is plain stupid. You must want that aeroplane awful bad."

"I want it," Ben said through gritted teeth. Murf and a roustabout had climbed into the net to untangle him. They weren't able to be gentle about it, not eight feet in the air with the crowd gawking all around them.

"Stay still," Murf said back in their tent. "Doc Epps says t'keep ice on your hock till the swelling goes down."

"What's a horse doctor know?"

"Only one we got, Ben. You'll be okay. Just pulled everything on that side too hard. Tell the truth, I'm more worried 'bout Fos. You know that guy still ain't showed up? Epps come back, but he don't even remember where he left Fos. Old Fos is drinking Parkton plumb dry!"

"He'd better show up after tomorrow's shot. That's when I'm buying the Wright."

"That dancer Clara asked how you are." Murf chuckled. "Derned if I don't think that big gal is sweet on you, Ben. You could get yourself something 'sides money for all the hurt you're getting."

He skipped breakfast. The pain wasn't worth it. After Murf had left for the mess tent, he heaved himself up against the aeroplane's skids and wobbled there panting. Lord, it hurt! After a few minutes, he hobbled outside to a stack of gasoline tins and sat against them for a long time soaking up the sun.

Finally Murf came back, chewing on a bun. "Bells afire! How bad are you?"

"Good enough."

"No, you ain't either. I'm going fer Rathrock."

Ben grabbed his sleeve. "Don't do that, Murf. I've got the whole day to get myself pulled together."

"I'm gonna do something. I can't leave you lying here like a crippled-up puppy. I'll tell Clara. She's a woman. They know 'bout sick people."

She came around the tent a few minutes later, jouncing with her peculiar walk, her feet kicking out her long gray muslin skirt. "Murf said—"

"I know what he said. I'm just resting until it passes."

Without invitation, she knelt and her fingers pressed his hip. He grunted.

"It won't pass if you just sit here."

"Doc Epps said it's a sprain, not a break."

"Then it should be soaked in cold water."

Ben flung out his arm, and even that hurt him. "Where am I going to find a bathtub around here!"

"Did you have breakfast?"

"Don't want any."

She brought him a mug of coffee and some scrambled eggs on a tin plate and made him eat. "Can you stand up?"

"If I don't have to walk far."

"I'll be back," she promised.

"I'm not going anyplace."

Murf walked out of the hangar tent wiping his hands on a rag. "She able to do anything fer you?"

"She's got some crazy idea about a bathtub."

"A bathtub! If that don't beat all."

A horse and wagon swung around the far side of the tent. Clara was in it. She jumped down and pulled Ben's arm across her solid shoulders. "Come on, Murf. Help me get him in the wagon."

She took the reins, and he hunched to one side to ease the jolts. The gray workhorse jogged out of the fairgrounds along a dirt lane toward a distant stand of willows. When the horse reached the trees, Ben saw that a creek ran behind them, screened from the lane by brush and high grass. Clara turned the buckboard off the road and they bounced along the creek bank.

She tied the reins to a sapling. He had to let her bear his weight, but she stood firm. They pushed through the reeds together. A narrow stretch of brown sand edged a pool beneath the willows. Clear water rippled through upstream rocks, then widened into eddies along the thin beach.

"Undress," Clara ordered. He stared at her. "Oh, come on, Ben. I have three brothers. Take off your coveralls and get into the water."

He stripped to his knee-length union suit, Clara steadying him as he struggled. The agony in his side made argument impossible. The stream was spring-fed, icy on his bare legs. He floundered in the soft creek bottom and fell on one knee.

"Oh, Lordy, you'll drown yourself!" She crossed her arms and pulled her dress over her head. Her cotton drawers and vest made her look more naked than the skimpy dancing costume ever had. Water swirled over her hips, and her powerful arm circled his waist. "Go out where it's deeper."

"It's cold!"

"That's what you need." When the frigid water was chest-high, she said, "Lean on me and move that leg around."

The water had stiffened him. He couldn't do it.

"Move your leg!" she insisted. "Lordy, you're helpless!" She ducked under, and her fingers closed around his thigh. He jumped. "That's right," she sputtered. Her hair was plastered across her face. She thrust it aside. "Move that leg!"

He forced himself to push his leg out in a slow underwater kick. Fierce pain shot through him, and he clutched her shoulder.

"Again. Don't stop."

He settled into an easy rhythm, shoving his leg forward, then swinging it behind him, flexing the knee until the pain was numbed in the cold water.

"Can you swim?"

"Of course!"

"Do it, then. I'm getting cold." She backed away, keeping a careful eye on him. "Swim!"

He struck out clumsily. He had grown used to the water, and his hip and leg had lost most of their stiffness. He plowed toward the far bank, then rolled over to drift in the cool stillness. On shore, Clara held her damp undergarments out from her body to dry in the warm breeze.

He tried standing again. To his surprise, his strained side held him well. "I'm coming out. You're pretty smart. The water's done me a lot of good."

She reached for his hand. "I'm all right now," he said, but she helped him anyway.

"You see? I knew what you needed. Lots of cold water. And some time away from everything. You're trying too hard to do too much at once."

"I'm trying to get the money for the aeroplane. All it takes is one more shot."

"And what will that do to you? What will the cannon do tonight?"

"It doesn't matter." He stepped toward the reeds, but she still held his hand.

"Ben, don't ever believe that the things you do don't matter."

11

Fos had finally shown up, crusty-eyed, with two days' stubble. He nodded sourly at Ben and Clara up on the wagon, then wobbled into the hangar tent.

"Been here 'bout an hour," Murf said quietly to Ben. "Just come in outta nowhere like he'd never been gone. You okay?"

Ben eased down from the buckboard by himself. He was feeling better. No doubt about that.

"I've got to get in costume," Clara said. "The show'll be starting soon. You be careful, Ben." She clicked the horse into a walk.

Murf squinted into the lowering sun. "You know something? That's quite a girl."

"Maybe."

"Bells afire, Ben! She's got you back on your feet. This morning, you wasn't worth a plugged nickel. Now you're ready to go at that cannon again, 'pears to me. I still say she's something."

"I'm interested in just one thing, Murf. The aeroplane."

"And when you set your mind on something, nobody'd better get in the way. You don't look right, left, and back, do you? Don't care who gets hurt."

"How am I hurting Clara?"

"To tell the truth, Ben, I wasn't thinking of Clara."

The sunset was blood red beneath the high clouds that had crept in from the southwest. Along the roadway from town came a great jam of autos and wagons and people on foot.

"The word's out good," Murf told Ben. "They're coming to see you kill yerself."

"How did *that* get started?"

"Only takes some talk in the right places. Rathrock had a couple of his people circ'late around telling how bad you was hurt last night, and saying you was bound and determined to make the final shot tonight whatever. They're sure coming, ain't they?"

At sundown, Clara brought Ben his coveralls, laundered and carefully chalked. He dressed in the hangar tent while Fos and Murf watched in silence. He tied the coveralls around his ankles and pulled his socks over the cords. When he straightened, a wave of blackness shut out his vision, and his head pounded. It passed quickly but left his knees wobbly. He clung to one of the tent poles. Murf started toward him, but Ben waved him off, then walked stiffly out of the tent.

He was unmistakable in the white garb. The crowd

122

parted for him. Children and their parents stared, but he ignored them. This was cheap glory. Anyone could do the shoot if he was desperate or stupid enough. There was little skill to it, he felt. Thanks to the gaudy posters, he had become Suicide Horner in just three days. No one seemed to remember that he was a flyer.

His walk up the midway was steady enough until he neared the cannon enclosure. The ugly muzzle stuck up above the canvas waiting for him. The gun was always waiting. Nothing hurt the gun. It was battering him to pieces but nothing happened to it at all. Its piston lost none of its punch. Its giant spring was just as powerful now as when Ben had made his first shoot. The cannon had killed Cordova. Tonight it waited to kill him.

He tried to force that thought out of his mind. In front of the ragged sideshow tent, he saw Clara and the other two dancers shimmying to the drumbeat, trying for a last tentful of rubes before the big event of the evening.

Rathrock was on the bally platform beside the ticket taker's stand, howling through his megaphone: "Tonight is your last chance—your one and only chance—to see Blasting Benjamin Horner fired from the mouth of a giant killer cannon into a net no bigger than a bed sheet!"

He spotted Ben. "And here he is, folks! Suicide Horner in person! Only a boy, but he's putting his life on the line just to give you the thrill you'll never forget. Come on up here, kid. Give the people a good look at nerves of steel, cool courage, sheer guts!"

Rathrock turned from the megaphone and bent down. "Get up here for a minute. It'll help fill the place."

Ben stared down into the gaping faces. They were real people, now, leathery farmers, pasty shopkeepers, hard women with tight lips, girls with pale, soft faces under summer bonnets, kids chewing popcorn. In there, in the enclosure with the cannon, they'd turn into a faceless mass hoping the big gun would kill him as it had murdered Cordova.

"In just minutes," Rathrock yammered, "you'll see something you will talk about the rest of your lives. With a mighty explosion, the killer cannon will blast this boy into empty space. Will he hit the net or will he smash into rock-hard mother earth like the man before him? This daredevil stunt has already killed one man, folks. Will it kill again tonight?"

He put his hand over the mouthpiece. "Don't pay any attention to this spiel, Ben. It's for the rubes. Strictly for the rubes."

Ben nodded, but Rathrock had shaken him just the same. "I'm going on in." Ben stepped down from the platform gingerly. The night air wasn't helping the hip any.

The cannon loomed above the torches, smelling the cool air, deciding what to do to him tonight. Little Max watched him climb onto the rear of the truck. "You okay, Ben? Shaky, I theenk."

"Let's get this over with."

Rathrock shoved through the crush at the entrance and trotted into the space the roustabouts held clear. His voice rose and fell as he swung the megaphone around the enclosure. The words didn't mean anything to Ben now. What mattered was the cannon.

He slapped the first rung, forced his fingers to close, and began the long climb up the monster's spine. He was jelly. Then he felt as if he were outside looking in at his own jittering body, watching his feet fumble on the rings. Could the crowd see that?

At the top, he looked beyond the high canvas fence. The

carnival had stopped. It held its breath along the midway and in front of the sideshow. The Little Egypt dancers stood frozen in place and stared up from their bally platform. He could see Clara's upturned white face.

He pulled his eyes away and looked far down the torchlit midway to the distant hangar tent. The Wright waited there, waited for him—if he lived through the next few minutes.

He doubled his legs beneath him and shoved his feet down the barrel. His hands slipped and he crashed down hard on the piston head. Beyond the muzzle, sound died. He could hear his own hard breathing.

What if he didn't give the signal? Suppose he simply failed to kick the barrel? Would anyone understand that twice had been enough, that it wasn't he who couldn't take it, but his body? He couldn't help what his body could or couldn't do. Max would ratchet the barrel down and they'd pull him out and the crowd would . . . would what? What could they do? Rathrock would give them their money back and tell Ben to get out of here. He wouldn't get the Wright, but he'd have his life.

He would say good-bye to Clara. Only to her. Not to Murf or Fos. They didn't care about him now. He wondered if they were out there. Before he had dropped down the muzzle, he had seen only Clara and the crowd, a giant faceless something waiting to see him mangled.

A taste of copper came into his throat. He had known all along what he was going to do. His left toe banged the bore's metal sheathing.

The distant *bung! bung!* was Max answering him. He tensed, arms quivering against his sides, face away from the bore. He shifted his weight—

The piston threw him upward. He felt the white flash

through the coveralls as the explosion thundered a fist of pain in his ears. The midway looped over his head. He hurtled sideways, the suddenly ferocious night wind ripping at him. The torches whirled in an orange spiral.

There was no net. No net at all. He was flying off into the sky, flying forever in a spin of glaring light with the echo of thunder in his head.

A web of hard wire battered him out of the air, put out the lights, silenced the noise. Then Murf's voice cut away the black cotton. "Ben! Ben! Don't touch him, folks. Might make it worse."

The moving blurs narrowed, came into focus. Ben lay on his back beside the net.

"I missed it," he gasped. "Hit the ground."

"You hit the net, awright," Murf said, "but near the edge. Then you flipped over the side. Can you sit up?"

His stomach jabbed at him with quick darts of pain, but he creaked up and leaned back with his hands flat in the dirt. "I don't think anything's busted."

"You come out of that gun at an angle and flopped sideways all the way across."

Ben remembered his last-minute shift in the cannon barrel. "Didn't have my weight the same on both legs. Makes a difference."

"Fine time to find that out. Can you get up?"

He lurched to his feet. His right side ached. The roustabouts shoved the crowd back. To Ben's amazement, the arena filled with cheers.

He threw both arms above his head. The crowd roared. He could see their faces again. An old man grinning. Women, fat and smiling. Farmers waving back.

"Hey!" Suddenly he roared with uncontrollable laughter, tears rolling down his face.

"Come on," Murf insisted. "Out this way." They ducked beneath the canvas skirt behind the net. Ben couldn't stop laughing and couldn't understand why Murf wasn't laughing with him.

"You'll be all right, I think," Murf's distant voice said.

"I'm fine. I'm fine," he giggled, struggling for breath.

"Let's get into the hangar tent." Murf said it as if Ben hadn't spoken at all.

The urge to laugh was overpowering. "I've got business with Rathrock," he managed. "Business." There was a weird madness in him, as if he were the only one to understand a huge joke. He shook off Murf's hand. "I'm going to see Rathrock."

He pulled himself up the entrance steps but found the carnival owner's wagon empty.

"You're looking for your dough already?" Rathrock had come off the midway and stood below him at the foot of the wagon steps. "Well, I got it right here. A bargain's a bargain. You did fine. Crazier'n a mule full of jimsonweed, but a showman. You want to keep on with that cannon stunt, you just—"

"You can take the cannon and—"

"Now hold on, Ben." Rathrock started up the steps, did something confusing with his hands, then looked at Ben closely. "I think you got a concussion there, Ben. One pupil's twice as big as the other. You better get yourself to bed."

"Just give me the money."

"It's in your hand, Ben."

He looked down. The ground swung toward him. He wanted to fall on it and sleep, but Rathrock's arm got in the way, caught him across the chest, then melted into soft blackness.

Ben came out of it staring straight up into luminous gray. He managed to focus his eyes on dirty canvas with the sun behind it. Without turning his head, he knew from the smell of gasoline and oil that he was in the hangar tent. He looked toward the ping of metal on metal.

" 'Bout time," Murf said from beneath the Wright's lower wing. "You awright? Got us some coffee here. Want some?" He poured Ben a cup and peered closely at him as he handed it over. "Sure you're awright?"

"I wish you'd stop saying that. I made it through the night, didn't I?" He sat up stiffly, then reached underneath himself to pull out an uncomfortable lump. It was the money Rathrock had paid him.

Murf eyed the wad of bills. "Fos says make sure your aeroplane is in good shape. So I'm making sure."

"Where is he?"

"Outside."

Fos sat on the stack of gasoline tins in the blinding sunshine, chewing a stalk of foxtail. He glanced sideways at Ben. "You all right?"

"Now it's unanimous. Yes, I'm all right. How about you?"

"You worried 'bout me? I thought all you worried 'bout was the aeroplane. You still want it?"

"If you'll sell it."

"Said I would. You got the money, it's yours."

"I've got the money." He counted it out on the gas tin at Fos's elbow. Behind him, Murf had come out of the tent to watch in silence. Fos shoved the bills in his pocket without looking at them.

"Guess that's that. I'll be leaving soon's I get my stuff together." The old flyer stood up, shoved his hands in his riding breeches and walked back into the tent.

"What about you, Murf?"

"What 'bout me?" He seemed surprised that Ben had asked. "I dunno 'bout me. Hate to think of ol' Fos heading outta here by hisself. What's he gonna do by hisself?"

"He'll have more'n two hundred bucks for himself after he gives you your share. He'd have a lot more if he hadn't drunk up everything he got from Rathrock."

"Yeah, but bells afire, you know Fos. He needs somebody."

"*I* need somebody to keep the Wright together, Murf. You know that old crock as well as you know Fos."

"I dunno. I dunno . . ."

"Look, I can't handle all this by myself!"

"Mebbe you shoulda thought of that sooner," Fos said, poking his head out of the tent. "Come on, Murf, I got your things here and your money."

"Murf?"

The string-bean mechanic looked over his shoulder at the Wright behind the partly rolled-up tent flap.

"Up to you, Murf," Fos said. "Mebbe the machine does need you more'n I do."

A distant shouting reached them from the midway. The wheel games and skill booths were warming up to work the afternoon crowd.

"The machine needs wrenches and screwdrivers," Murf said, "but it doesn't care who's hanging on the other end. Ben's learned enough to keep her wheezing awhile. I'll leave him my tools, Fos. Let's get moving."

"I need *you*, Murf," Ben implored. A little edge of panic began to cut into his self-confidence.

"Uh-uh, Ben. You don't need anybody. Least not so's I can see it. You rolled right over us since you first joined up. Well, you got yourself the aeroplane. But that's all you got. Come on, Fos." He took his duffel from Fos and walked toward the old lizzie.

Unexpectedly, Fos stuck out his hand. "No hard feelings, Ben. You only done what you thought was right. I'm no stunt flyer. Always said that, didn't I?" He smiled thinly. "Heerd there was some auto racing getting started near Chicago. Some fella building a track outta wood. 'Magine that! Got half a mind to go on up there, see what it's all 'bout. Wish you luck, Ben. You get some rough edges knocked off, you'll be one heckuva flyer. A lot better'n me."

He trotted after Murf, not looking back, taking only his little bag of personal belongings and leaving Murf's battered metal toolbox beside the gas tins.

That's not much to show for what they've done, Ben thought. Two bags of worn-out clothes, couple of nicked razors, what they've got on their backs. And about five hundred dollars, plus whatever Murf had saved out of his Rathrock cut. But they had something else, he realized, something between them that he hadn't been able to break up. How much was that worth?

"Maybe I'll wish I'd kept the money," Ben muttered aloud, but he didn't believe it, certainly not after the flying show he put on that hazy afternoon. The old engine ran like a fine watch. Murf had seen to that. He was gone, but what he had done for the battered engine stayed with Ben. The air was smooth and buoyant. The Wright responded instantly the moment Ben made the control movements.

He pulled daring vertical banks over the crowd, flew close enough to blow their hats off, and climbed past five hundred feet to cut the engine and spiral down without power, landing with the propellers dead as sticks. The spectators went wild.

It was easy! Just like he'd always told Fos. He and a borrowed roustabout pushed the aeroplane back into the hangar tent. No problem at all. He could make enough money by next spring to buy a much better machine, maybe a Wright Baby Grand. They were fast. With an aeroplane like that, he could even try some of the big air meets. He was getting impatient at being tied to a two-bit carnival for show dates and locations. Now that he was operating the aeroplane on his own, maybe the time was drawing close to when he would be truly independent.

In midweek, Max left the carnival, taking the cumbersome cannon truck toward St. Louis, where he hoped to find a buyer. Before noon the next day, Rathrock's faded flatcars were hauled out of the Mt. Olive depot behind a chartered locomotive, heading westward for a swing through Missouri as long as the late summer weather held out.

With the tool kit and his suitcase strapped to the passenger seat, Ben lifted the Wright out of the fairgrounds and followed the train west. Next stop, Higbee along the Rocher Pierre River. After a two-day stand there, the outfit was moving down the Missouri, Kansas & Texas Railroad for a full week in Clinton. Rathrock had begun to work them southward. Fall weather was coming.

Near the grandstand during the last day at Mt. Olive, Ben had found a discarded Chicago paper. The front-page story about an air show to be scheduled soon in Hammond, Indiana, had made his mind spin. An *air* show! A whole show devoted to flying certainly had more to offer than Rathrock's sad little wandering carnival. He would stick with Rathrock a while longer, but the first time the carnival operator got in his way, Ben was pulling out to track down that air show. In his heart, he hoped that day wasn't far off.

12

In Higbee, Ben paid too much attention to the crowd and not enough to his landing. The Wright dropped from three feet high onto the hard sun-cooked mud flat and an axle snapped. He took the pieces to the blacksmith tent and surprised the carnival smithy with his own skill; surprised himself, in fact. Uncle Alex had taught him well. The Wright was back in the air without missing a performance.

Four days later in Clinton, the long chain drive to the left propeller outrigger jumped its sprocket just as he began his takeoff run. The Wright slewed sharply left and galloped toward the crowd. He cut the switch just in time and sat shaking in the seat, sweat pouring down his sides. Close, too close. But by late afternoon, he had made the repair, had taken the slack out of both chains, and the Wright rose easily on the cooling air.

At the end of the surprisingly successful week in Clinton, the weather turned raw. Rathrock sniffed the air like an old coonhound, his bad eye blinking in the biting wind. "That's it. That's winter coming. We'll beat it to Arkansas, then it's anybody's guess. Maybe they'll put out a few bucks to see us down in Louisiana bayou country after that."

"So where do we go from here?" Ben asked.

"Boarville."

Ben dug out a map Fos had given him weeks ago and found Boarville in the northeastern corner of Arkansas— more than two hundred miles across the two-thousand-foot-high Ozark Plateau. Ben wasn't about to fly over that territory. He demanded that Rathrock lend him two of the more skillful roustabouts, and in half a day, they dismantled the Wright's outer wing panels. The carnival pulled out of Clinton with the aeroplane staked to a flatcar.

It was in Arkansas that the disaster that so many of the carnies had felt in their bones finally struck. The train rattled into Boarville through a deluge. Rathrock's Carnival Cavalcade huddled in the wagons lashed on the old flatcars. Nobody would lift a finger until Rathrock chased them out into the downpour a little after dawn.

They unloaded into a quagmire along the siding north of the tired clapboard town a quarter mile down the wagon road. The horses steamed in the muggy air and roustabouts cursed each other and everything around them.

"How am I supposed to get the Wright out of here?" Ben fumed. "It tows all right on a hard road, folded up like this, but the wheels are too narrow for this mud."

He hit Rathrock with that at a bad time. "That's your

problem," the carnival operator snapped at him from one of the tackle flatcars. "Should of thought about that before you let everybody walk out on you."

"Look, Rathrock, the rain isn't my fault. Let me borrow one of your wagons."

"It'll take a heavy-duty rig, and I don't have a spare heavy-duty rig. Work it out yourself. That's what you wanted. I got a hundred people on my back. I didn't make this lousy weather, either."

In an hour, the ragged line of wagons pulled out for the fairgrounds, horses churning the road to pudding. Ben knew he'd never make it out there now. He watched them disappear around a steep hillside, and he slapped a folded top wing panel in frustration.

The rain stopped abruptly, and a scattering of idlers slogged up the main drag from town. They gathered around the folded aeroplane and stared in silence.

"What is it?" a burly farmer finally asked, his thumbs hooked under the bib straps of his overalls. "Newfangled farm machinery?"

"Shucks, Cornwall," another man laughed. "Thet's one of them flyin' machines. Busted up real bad."

"Folded up," Ben said. "It flies, if I could find a way to get it to the fairgrounds. Any of you got a spare wagon?"

"Thet'd bust up a wagon. Where's the flyer?"

"I'm the flyer."

"Yo're funnin' us!"

"If there was a way to get this thing out of here, you'd see soon enough. Somebody's got to have a heavy wagon in this burg."

"Nobody's got a wagon fer you, so whyn't you *fly* out of here, sonny!" A chorus of hoots greeted the suggestion.

"If I can't even get the thing off the flatcar, how do you think I'm going to get it off the ground? And from where?"

"How 'bout Leroy's field? Jest through the woods there. It's allus the first to drain off. We all could shove the machine through the wagon path."

That was a better idea than anybody else had given him this morning. "I'll have to take a look first."

They led him to the trail through the thin woods. The passage wasn't wide, but it was straight, and a carpet of pine needles gave the soft ground some substance. "Leroy's field" was slightly crowned, sandy and solid with closely cut hay bristle.

In a confused gaggle, the whole gang of them manhandled the folded aeroplane off the flatcar, down the gluey roadway to the path through the woods, then along the hundred-foot trail to the edge of the field. By this time, Leroy Piggott himself was on hand, a red-jowled giant of a man with a bottom like an overloaded hammock.

Ben sent the older boys back for a few tins of gasoline from the local garage where he'd spotted the familiar red-and-white Standard Oil sign. The others helped him spread out the wings.

"Watch it, there!" he found himself hollering. "You can put your hand right through that covering. . . . Take it easy with those spars. They're just bamboo!" Had Fos and Murf ever gone through *this*?

The boys reappeared with three large cans of gas in a wheelbarrow. He poured the clear fluid through the piece of chamois Murf had taught him to use as a filter to strain out any grit or water in the gas.

The crowd kept changing as the men went off to their fields or their jobs in town. He had mostly small boys now, and a scattering of men who didn't seem to worry about working. The sun was high by the time he had adjusted the last rigging-wire turnbuckle and tied the tool kit to the passenger seat. He'd been careful to promise no rides as rewards for helping him. He wanted to get to the fair-grounds without further complications because now it looked as if he might make it after all.

He set the engine adjustments and walked around the wings to pull the right-hand propeller himself. He could never ask a bystander to do that. The chain-interlocked propellers were deadly when they began turning.

The engine was balky from dampness, then it popped black smoke and caught so unexpectedly that he nearly slipped beneath the swishing blade. He raced around the wings and scrambled into the pilot's seat.

The echoing bark swelled the crowd. More people dashed through the woods. He motioned all of them out of the way, buckled Cordova's white helmet beneath his chin, pulled the goggles into place, and advanced the throttle lever.

The machine began to roll across the soggy turf. There was no wind, so his takeoff direction didn't matter. Engine howling, the old Wright labored up the rise of the field's crown, slowly picking up speed.

The far end of the field came into view, still a half mile distant. Ben stared. Out there, the field flattened into a creek, spread wide and coffee-colored from the rain. The creek's far bank wasn't anything like the gentle slope on this side. It jutted up in a wall twenty feet high, a clay-faced cliff topped with a scraggle of stunted pines.

He began to feel wind in his face, but not the solid blast of lift-off speed. The Wright rocked across the field's crown and gained speed on the slight downslope. Ben leaned into the rushing air, pleading for lift.

The cliff grew higher, towered above the burbling creek water. Then he felt the first lightness in the wings. He inched back the elevator lever. The aeroplane rose, then clumped back to earth as the trailing ends of the wheel skids dragged furrows behind him. More carefully this time, he eased the thick lever back again. The four wheels bounced free.

The creek bank raced toward him, its gray and brown markings in clear detail. He fought the panic to haul the front of the machine high. That would lead to quick loss of flying speed and a stall that would pitch him uncontrollably to the ground. He held the machine level, building up speed, heading straight for the embankment.

Hold it down . . . hold it down . . . Fos, what would you say now? How did I get into this? I should have walked all the way out to the crown of the field, not taken their word about what was on the other side.

The massive bank was close! He hauled back the elevator lever. The Wright nosed up, mushed forward, then the ground began to drop. The creek rolled beneath him. The bank fell away.

The aeroplane lifted higher, but not quite high enough. Its wheels slammed through the pine tops. Then she broke clear and climbed smoothly. He craned his neck to look for damage, but there was none. A small miracle! Maybe things were going to work out, after all.

He owed the townspeople something, even if they had refused to lend him a wagon. He banked steeply, swung back over the creek, and let the Wright sink below the field's crown, its wheels not a foot above the sod. The little cluster of people burst into view as he topped the rise. They waved, then suddenly scattered as he pulled over them, clearing the trees by a few feet.

A surprise awaited him on the other side of the thin woods. Curving back into Boarville from the south road was a line of wagons, badly spaced, a ragtag bunch that could only be Rathrock's Carnival Cavalcade!

He swung over the caravan. Only a few faces glanced

upward. There was a look of dejection about the whole mud-spattered wagon train.

Ben landed without trouble and ran back through the woods to find Rathrock.

"First time this has ever happened!" the chunky carnival operator fumed, his left eye winking wildly. "Sheriff shows up, asks for a hundred bucks from me and ten bucks from each midway game. *A hundred bucks!*"

"You've paid off before," Ben said.

"Ten bucks, maybe twenty. But this guy's a highway robber. I couldn't let him get away with that. The word'd spread like prairie fire. 'Hit up Rathrock. He'll pay whatever you want to nick him for.' Why, that kind of thing would clean bust me! We're clearing out of this burg soon's I can get the railroad to send back an engine."

"But I just got the Wright set up. You saw it up there. That took four, almost five hours."

"So that's your share of the bad luck, Ben. Unless you want to fly to the next stop, take it right back down again. I'll have those two razorbacks give you a hand."

"Where's the next stop?"

"I don't know yet."

"Then how the devil am I supposed to fly there?"

"Ben, I just don't know. It's not my problem. Fly along with the train or something. I got a whale of a lot more on my mind than you and that aeroplane."

Ben's temper soared. "All right. All right! You're not doing me any good, not when you let some tin-badge sheriff push you out of town. Not when you won't even tell me where you're going from here!"

"For Pete's sake, Ben, I just said I don't know where—"

"I'm leaving. You don't owe me anything, and I don't owe you anything. Clean break, Rathrock. I quit!" He had run out of words and stood beside the office wagon, hands balled into fists, his breath coming hard.

Rathrock gazed at him coldly. "I don't think I had that coming. You aren't a very patient kind of fella, are you, Ben? But if that's the way you want it, that's the way you got it. Good luck." He strode off to shout at the nearest roustabouts.

So that's that, Ben thought, his anger fading. What had gotten into him? Things had been bad before. It was the combination, he decided. No wagon, no help, nearly smashing up on takeoff, and now Rathrock telling him to knock the Wright back down again. He was sorry they'd parted in a flurry of hard words, but there wasn't going to be any backing down. He didn't need Rathrock. He could make more money on his own.

He should have made the break sooner, in Missouri, not down here in Nowhere, Arkansas. Flying to Hammond from here would be as wild a stunt as being shot out of the cannon. But that had been in the back of his mind since Mt. Olive, he realized. A long cross-country flight was a hare-brained idea, a wild scheme. . . .

But he'd do it! If the old Wright would hang together for him, he would do it! He had enough money for gas and oil, money he'd made at Clinton. The trip would begin right here and now. He tramped back to Leroy Piggott's field.

A little knot of Boarville people watched him lash the extra gas tins on the lower wing. When he'd finished, he noticed a woman standing apart from the crowd. Gray dress, no hat. She had a drab carpetbag at her feet.

"Ben?" she called. The woman at the edge of the woods was the Little Egypt dancer, Clara Dembrowski. "I heard you quit, Ben." News traveled like electricity through Rathrock's bunch. "I quit, too."

He stared down from his wing perch. "You quit? Why?"

"The whole thing is coming apart. Bernice and Floss told me it always does this time of year. Rathrock heads into Louisiana or Mississippi. Some of the people stay with him to play the potato towns along the Gulf. They make just enough to keep from starving until next season. That's not for me. I don't want to have to do what Bernice and Floss say they do to make money." She looked at the ground, then back up. "What about you, Ben?"

"I'm heading for northern Indiana. There's a big air show at Hammond. I'm not sure this old box kite'll get me there, but I'm going to try." He jumped to the ground and picked up his old suitcase, tying it into the passenger's seat as Clara watched in silence.

When he finished, she said, almost in a whisper, "Ben, take me with you."

He frowned. "Take you along? I don't need anybody with me."

She laid her hand on his arm. "Ben, you do need somebody. You can't cut yourself off from everyone like you've been doing. There used to be three of you. Now there's just you."

"Fos and Murf wanted to try auto racing."

"All that's left is just you," she repeated.

He looked into her wide face. Her eyes were pleading, but he turned away. "No. I might not even make it myself." He didn't need a dumb farm girl turned carnival dancer. She'd only be added weight. And a lot of weight, at that. People complicated things. He didn't need anybody at all.

The engine, still warm, caught on his second pull. He ducked beneath the skid wires, boosted himself into the flyer's seat, and planted his muddy shoes on the crossbar.

"Ben?" Her voice reached him over the engine's grumble. He shoved the throttle wide open. The Wright began to roll. It bounded up the field's slope and kept rising. The field fell behind, and the aeroplane cleared the bank by a good hundred feet. He brought the machine around and howled over the depot, dipping his wings left, then right. A salute for you, Lucien Rathrock. Maybe more than you would do for me.

Then he saw Clara, tiny at the edge of Leroy's field, her hand raised in a little wave. Taking her with him wouldn't have worked, Ben told himself. It just wouldn't have worked.

He put the afternoon sun behind him and let the air blast push him back in the seat. He didn't need Fos or Murf or Rathrock or Clara Dembrowski. He didn't need anybody. He was free now, and on the move.

13

The wind burned hard against his face. The engine sang behind him, and the old Wright rode the sea of air with an ease that he'd never felt before. Was it the gentle afternoon, flat calm after this morning's rain? Was it because he had logged enough flying hours to know that he'd truly mastered the machine?

No, it wasn't the smoothly running machine or the fine weather that gave him this great feeling of release. It was that he was finally and truly on his own. Fos Pepperidge and his bottle, Murf and his little sermons were in the past. He was out from under Rathrock and his sleazy show.

God, it was wonderful to be up here, hundreds of feet above it all, slipping through crystal-clear air and depending on nobody but himself. He had proved something, hadn't he! If you looked out for yourself and didn't worry too much about the other fellow's problems—didn't let him get in your way—then you got pretty much what you wanted.

He had the aeroplane now, just as he'd planned. And he was heading for a real air show, not the ragtag kind of flying Fos had insisted on, but a genuine show with professional pilots. He laughed into the wind. The old drunk was really out of it now. He was probably guzzling down the money Ben had paid him as fast as he could buy whiskey with it. There was no hope for people like that.

The engine didn't skip a beat all the way to the Mississippi. He sighted the river's big loops an hour after takeoff. The land along the river was as desolate as had been the forty miles of timberland eastward from Boarville, but there were some flat areas, too.

He ran out of sun just as he spotted a tiny river town on the Missouri side. He cut back power and glided into a hay field south of the settlement. A lean, worked-out farmer in his sixties loped out of a weather-battered house along the north edge of the field, half crazy with excitement at seeing his first "airyplane."

Ben was in luck. The farmer was lonely, and so was his bone-thin wife. Ben shared their beans and bread and was given a room in the back of the house.

He was off again just after daylight, first pouring the extra gas through the chamois-covered funnel into the tank slung on the struts over the engine.

The machine lifted eagerly in the cool, buoyant river-bottom air, pulling easily above the banks before he'd gone half a mile. He held the Wright in a climb until the engine labored, let her settle a hundred feet or so, then began cutting across the river's broad loops.

At midmorning, the engine began to run rough. Ben nursed it along until he spotted a farm with an automobile parked nearby. He circled the pasture, flew low to herd the cows into one end, then dropped in gently. The flabbergasted farmer sold him a tinful of gasoline right out of his battered Moline Dreadnought auto. Ben checked the engine, but he found nothing more significant than moisture dripping off the carburetor. Some water in the gas, that was all, he decided. He was back in the air in thirty minutes, certain he had left the farmer itching to get into town with his story.

Cairo came up on schedule, exhaling a blue haze above the joining of the Mississippi and Ohio rivers, buffeting the Wright with rising warm currents when Ben headed over the south end of town. He changed course quickly and made a northeastward sweep across the mile-wide waterway, striking out over the flats south of the Ohio.

Twenty minutes later, the engine died with no warning whatever. One minute, it was firing away at his elbow. The next, there was a horrifying silence.

Ben jiggled the throttle. Dead. The twin propellers clanked to a stop behind him, their linkage chains rattling in the wind. He dropped the machine into a glide.

The land below was raw and brush-covered without a building in sight. He looked around frantically. There were perhaps three hundred feet to go, and the Wright was dropping fast, wind whistling through her rigging. Then, far ahead, Ben spotted a field, probably a once-flooded area with new grass beginning to put hide back on the baldness. If he tried to stretch out the glide, perhaps he couldn't make it. The machine was moving down faster than it drifted forward.

He remembered his first exhibition flight, the awful moment when he thought he was going to smash into the cornfield. He thrust the control lever forward. The ground flew upward, but he gained valuable speed. He eased the machine back into a fast, flat glide. Brush scudded beneath the wings. A treetop slapped the wheels. He held the Wright steady, sweat creeping under his helmet. Then the stretch of thin grass rolled under him. The wheels scrubbed the ground, and he was down.

He sat frozen, the cooling engine ticking behind him. Was this a crazy idea, after all? Was it really possible to fly nearly five hundred miles all by himself, with no ground crew, spare parts, or even somebody at the other end knowing he was supposed to get there? No use sitting here wondering, he told himself. He had to do something about it.

The engine trouble was all too obvious: a crimped water hose. The rubber had rotted and closed up, overheating and seizing the engine. He could shorten the hose and remove the rotted section.

The repair wasn't quite that easy. The interior of the hose had crumbled at the crimp, and he found particles all through the cooling system. He had to drain the radiator, and he needed water. A stream he remembered gliding over when he landed turned out to be a good mile distant.

The sun was low when he finally got everything back together and wiped his hands on a rag from the toolbox. He untied his two thin blankets and spread them on the ground beneath the wings. A thin mist rose off the flats, muffling the cricket chirps and chilling him. He set his jaw and fought for sleep. Nothing was going to stop him. Nothing! Not bad gasoline or rotten water hoses or freezing out here on the Kentucky flats.

At daybreak, the engine took a lot of turning to get the

dampness out of its system, but at last it chugged into life in a cloud of blue oil smoke. He pulled the Wright into the heavy morning air and headed into the sun.

He recrossed the Ohio northwest of Paducah, where the river looped down past the sprawled city, then swung north to glitter among the hills ten miles ahead. An hour later, a change in the engine's clatter twisted Ben in his seat.

The hose, which he had repaired by shortening it, had vibrated loose. Water poured from the bottom of the long vertical radiator, then was whipped into spray by the air blast behind the wings.

He dropped fast, looking desperately for a field long enough for a landing. Then he spotted a road that wound eastward through the wooded countryside. It offered a straight stretch about a half mile long just past a small farm.

He banked steeply, lost too much altitude, and flattened out to save as much height as he could. The engine heated rapidly and began to labor. He cut it off and wind began to shrill through the rigging wires. The road drifted closer. He turned, lined up on its straight portion, and pumped the control lever to fishtail away the final hundred feet.

The cumbersome biplane hit hard, bounced with a snap, then stayed down much too heavily. The lower wing tips sliced off roadside goldenrod and burdock and tossed them in the air.

Ben was out and checking the damage the instant the machine stopped rolling. The left skid was split. He could probably fix it well enough with electrical tape, but he needed new hose, water, and a tin or two of gasoline.

The house, a mile-long walk south, was part of a small truck farm run by a woman as tough as an oak knot, dressed in weathered bib overalls and a sweat-stained straw hat. "Flyer, y'say? Was that what went sailin' over my head while back? Shore ain't here to stay, air they? You got an airyplane, but now you gotta borry my horse and wagon to git it goin'!"

She sounded angry but turned out to be laughing at him. "Take the rig, boy. General store's 'bout four miles past where you set down."

He found new hose there, and bacon and eggs, which the grocer let him cook on the potbellied stove to a chorus of jokes from the local hangers-around. He filled one of his tins with water from the store's pump, the other with auto gas, fixed the radiator line and the skid, returned the horse and wagon, and was back in the air just past noon.

The sky had heated unevenly and was lumpy beneath puffy clouds. The Wright thudded through turbulence for an uncomfortable hour before the air smoothed over flattening country. The clouds had grown together and hid the sun. He passed high over the junction where the Ohio, winding thickly toward the distant blue smudge that was Evansville, was joined by the narrower Wabash. Here he swung north to bisect the smaller river's loops.

Perhaps fifteen miles to the west, the sky had darkened ominously. Thunderstorm! He had to get down.

Anxiously, he looked for a town. He was tired and wanted to sleep under a roof if he could. A white church spire five miles ahead caught his eye. He turned toward it, pushing the engine harder. The first gusts in advance of the storm rocked the machine. He found a cut-over wheat field at the edge of the settlement, dropped in without circling, and as soon as he stopped rolling, tore open the toolbox. He snatched up the three sharpened hickory stakes and the coil of rope Murf had put in there three weeks before.

With a rock he pounded the stakes deep beneath the wing tips and tail and tied the machine down. The rising wind threw rain across the wings. A handful of people had begun to trot up the main drag toward him, but the onrushing storm made them hesitate, then break for cover. Ben tugged his suitcase from under its lashings and dashed along the street as blue-white lightning flashed and volleys of thunder shook store windows. He made it to the Muncie House just as hard rain drenched the street.

He was away again in the early morning and was rattling over Wallsville in midafternoon. In the distance, to the northeast, Ben saw the riverfront of Vincennes, the narrow ribbon of the Wabash rimming the city's near edge. Somewhere just beyond the horizon's blue rim lay Clarkston and Alex Horner's smithy. He shook his head. No, he was finished with all that. He was a flyer now, and he had no need for Uncle Alex.

He swung the machine around and spotted a farm with a tractor on the Illinois side of the river. Tractors meant gasoline. The farm had two barns, both heavily whitewashed, an assortment of outbuildings, and a house that jutted up from the Illinois flatlands slab-sided and three stories tall. Ben circled and watched a man come out of one of the barns and shade his eyes against the sun. He cut the power and bounced into the pasture near the barns, sending a chestnut mare galloping to the far end of the field.

The negotiation for a night's lodging and enough gas for the tank and an extra tinful took only a few minutes. The farmer and his wife were overcome by the novelty of it all.

In the morning, the sun was hidden by ground fog. The old machine bumped forward as if it were reluctant to try this last leg of the flight—the two-hundred-mile pull to Hammond all in one shot. Then it rose out of the pasture in a gentle turn, left the fog layer below, and soared into clean cold air.

Ben grinned. The big-name flyers had nothing on him!

He had already flown almost three hundred miles, and today he was going to eat up two hundred more in one northward pull.

At noon, he landed near the Illinois town of Williamsport to refill the gas tank. The trip today had been so uneventful that he was almost disappointed. Then the radiator spewed rusty spray all the way across the Iroquois River, and he sweated into a field near Rensselaer, more than ten miles off course.

He spent the rest of that day and all of the next three struggling to force auto hose over the engine and radiator fittings, and he wasn't in the air until early Saturday.

He flew right into the meet while he was still looking for it. An aeroplane appeared out of nowhere and swept past him on the left, jerking Ben's head around. The machine had a single stubby wing set well forward, with the circular engine just ahead of it. The narrow fuselage was enclosed in back of the tandem seats. Open boxwork supported the underslung rectangular elevator and jaunty rudder.

A Blériot! He'd seen pictures of the fast French machines. Louis Blériot had crossed the English Channel in one back in 1909, and the design was still speedier by far than any aeroplane Ben could think of that was built in America. The monoplane with its lone flyer pulled away in a climb. Ben leaned forward and looked down.

Near a road that arrowed south from the distant city of Hammond, a row of gray and white tents marked the air-meet site. A dozen aeroplanes were parked along the tent line. He could make out a scattering of people around the machines. Behind the tents, a big dirt parking area was dotted with a few automobiles. A group of spectators ranged along the rope line extending from the hangar tents, but it was just a lonely little straggle. Some crowd! This wasn't impressive at all. Still, it was barely noon.

A shadow flicked over him. The Blériot was back, sailing in behind him in a flat dive, then waltzing ahead like an insolent bird waving its tail feathers in his face. The flyer, sitting high in the narrow forward seat, twisted around to grin and then taunt him with a wave.

He had never shared the sky with anyone before. At all the towns Rathrock's Carnival Cavalcade had played, he'd never seen another flying machine. He was fascinated and oddly challenged.

The other flyer looked back again, then the Blériot sank away to the right. A game of tag? All right, if that was what the idiot wanted! Ben thrust the Wright into a dive and followed the monoplane.

It was hopeless. The Wright was a box kite, held back by the drag of a dozen struts and all the baggage he carried. The wind began to squeal through the wing bracing, and he throttled back.

The Blériot leaped up, swung around, and danced behind him before he could reverse his controls and pull the Wright out of its downward slant. The Blériot hung back there, its goggled flyer grinning behind the propeller's shimmer.

Too close for comfort, Ben thought, his head swiveling like a turkey's in a trap. He yanked the wing warping lever. The Wright's left panels rose high above Lake Michigan, lying leaden on the north horizon. The biplane slid to the right, but the Blériot stuck like flypaper.

Ben heaved on the warping lever again. The Wright lay over to the left, slipping away a hundred feet before he leveled out. The Blériot snarled closer to his tail.

The other machine was faster, but maybe he could use his own slowness to his advantage. He began to ease back the power, bringing the front of the machine higher to compensate for loss of lift. The Wright mushed forward on the edge of a stall. Over the grumble of his engine, he heard the Blériot snort and backfire.

The French machine wallowed in the air, its wings warping alternately in quick jerks to stay level. Then the nose dropped. The faster machine sailed beneath him, and Ben looked down into its front cockpit. He could see the flyer's arms working the controls and the white goggled face staring up at the lumbering Wright.

Ben brought the engine back to full life, headed down steeply, and managed to ride the Blériot's tail for a few seconds. The monoplane's rudder flapped at him playfully, then the machine pulled away and left him chasing empty air.

He was tired of the one-sided game. He throttled the engine and let the Wright settle in a lazy circle over the big air-meet field. The roadway drifted toward him, flicked beneath his wheels. The Wright bumped along the tie-down line, its engine blurping unevenly. He taxied to the end of the line and cut the engine.

A few idlers wandered toward him, but were brushed aside by a sunburned little man who wore golfing knicker-bockers and a checkered cap. He opened a leather notebook, ran a pencil down a page, and looked up. "Name?"

"Ben Horner."

"Where from, Horner? I don't see you listed in preregis-trations."

"Indiana, Arkansas, anywhere. Take your pick." Ben flipped a thumb toward the sparse row of aeroplanes. "Looks like you could use anybody who shows up."

The official snapped his notebook shut and stuck his pencil over his ear. "Can't argue with you. See McElroy. That tent at the end of the line. He's running the show. If McElroy says you're in, you're in."

The open-fronted tent was a picture of gloom. Ben could see it in the faces of the men clustered around the registration table. "Who's McElroy?" he said into the silence. Behind him, he heard the Blériot's engine blipping on its landing approach.

"I am." The moustached air-show promoter slumped in a camp chair behind the table. He looked like Farragut discovering that he should have paid attention to the torpedoes after all. His sharp eyes, set close together and deep over bony cheeks, flicked out at Ben, then dismissed him.

Ben said, "I'd like to register." Outside, the Blériot's bicycle wheels clumped to the turf.

McElroy's narrow eyes swung back. "As what? You brought in that old kite? Fat lot of good that'll do us." He ran long shaky fingers along the edge of his pointed jaw. "We need Beachey and we get—who are you?"

"Ben Horner."

"We get Ben Horner."

"Jeez, Mac," one of the men around the table said, pulling at the end of his bristly blond moustache, "take what you can get. This thing's going right down the chute the way things stand now."

Leonard McElroy sighed. "Simmons, when you build around Beachey, advertise around Beachey, then Beachey don't show up, you just don't sign anybody on and hope he'll save you."

"Why not? We're gonna get lynched if a real crowd shows up. More flyers we got, the harder it'll be to catch us."

"Sign him on," said a girl's voice behind Ben. "I have a feeling he's got something."

14

The girl who had just entered was a little thing in riding breeches, boots, and a close-fitting leather jacket. A smile danced across her round face, and she tossed her loose brown hair back from her forehead impatiently. "You're really something, Mac! This isn't Rheims or Dominguez field. Gordon Bennett never heard of this meet. You're trying to do two things at once, and you're bungling both of them."

The others listened seriously to this stormy girl. Then Ben noticed the red goggle marks around her snapping ginger-colored eyes and the windburn on her cheeks.

"Two things like what?" McElroy said icily.

"Like trying to run a high-class competitive air meet, which the public is tired of watching, and at the same time trying to make a circus out of it with Lincoln Beachey as the main attraction, and without whom you are in real trouble."

McElroy seemed to crumple. "So what do I do, Bunny? Fold up my tents? I'm only trying to sign on some flyers who know what they're doing."

"You've got twelve aeroplanes. Thirteen if you sign on—" She turned to Ben. "What's your name?"

"Horner."

"If you sign on Horner. I know he can fly. He's the only one here who could get on my tail for even a few seconds. That was pretty smart," she said to Ben, "slowing up like that. You knew the Blériot would stall if I stayed behind you. Sign him on!" she snapped at McElroy.

The meet promoter looked into the impassive faces around him. "Where you been flying, Horner?"

"Illinois, Missouri, downstate." He felt good here among real flyers, though he was stunned to find one of them was a girl. "Mostly with a carnival."

"Carnival? What kind of flying is that?"

"Exhibition."

McElroy studied the papers on the table. "Exhibition. You got a . . ." He leaned forward to peer down the line of aeroplanes. "Exactly what is that thing?"

"Wright Model B."

"Built when?"

"In 1909, I think."

"Looks a lot older than that."

"It's had a tough life," Ben said. "I just flew it in from Arkansas."

Someone in the crowd of flyers whistled.

154

"Damn!" McElroy marveled. "That's maybe three hundred miles!"

"Closer to five hundred," Ben said. "That old crock's held together with spit and fence wire."

He signed the sheet McElroy thrust at him. The girl had walked outside to talk with the official in golf clothes. "Who's she?" Ben asked the promoter.

McElroy looked shocked. "You don't recognize Bunny Daye? She's big stuff around these parts. One of the first women to fly, along with Blanche Scott and Harriet Quimby. She's good, too. It's not just the Blériot."

Ben walked out to her. "McElroy gives you quite a write-up. Thanks for putting in a good word for me."

"I'm just trying to keep this little turkey shoot in business," she said. "Where'd you learn to fly that old kite?" Her voice had a high-pitched ring, as if she were ready to break into a laugh.

"You wouldn't believe it if I told you. Is there someplace around here to get something to eat?"

They found a refreshment stand behind the hangar tents at the edge of the big parking lot. He bought them sandwiches and bottles of ginger beer. "Where'd you find the Blériot?"

"Bought it in South Bend from a man who thought he was going to make a fortune in the aeroplane business. He imported six of them, then he practically had to give them away. American flyers don't trust monoplanes."

"You do."

"Half the world does," Bunny said. "Europe's full of them. It's the oddest thing. We invented the aeroplane nine years ago, then we let the French and English go right past us. They've flown almost a hundred miles an hour! We haven't done much more than the Wright Brothers did at Kitty Hawk."

He took a quick pull from his soft-drink bottle. "Cal Rodgers and Bob Fowler flew across the whole country. Lincoln Beachey got the aeroplane to do what nobody thought it could."

"But we're still flying antiques. You see what's here. Some other Wright B's, a Wright EX, which is no more than a single-seat B, some Curtiss pushers, two Baldwins. They're all biplanes with pusher engines and a forest of struts and wires. All the same. All swiped from the original Wright designs. My Blériot makes them look sick."

"What's the difference? They all fly. That's what people come to see."

"You're making the same mistake Mac's making. The public wants to see something different. Around here, they've had their fill of point-to-point races and height records and endurance contests. But they'll always come out to watch flyers risk their necks doing stunts."

Ben looked at the nearly deserted parking lot. "Then why aren't they here?"

"Because Mac's always run the other kind of show. To him, a meet is a sportsmen's contest with all kinds of rules. That was good enough a year ago, but now it isn't. That's why he wanted Beachey here. One daredevil act to draw the crowd for his gentlemen's contest."

Ben said, "I can't tell whose side you're on."

"Oh, that's not hard. I'm on aviation's side. I want to see progress. If an air meet helps aviation, I'm on that side. If it's a sideshow, I don't think that's much help at all. But I love flying and I'm here, and that's all I expect anyone to understand."

Ben finished the ginger beer and wiped his mouth with the back of his hand. "I think I understand."

"No man does. I'm twenty and on my own. I have my own aeroplane. I can fly as well as any of you."

"Better," Ben said. "You made me look like a pelican up there."

She thought that over, then grinned. "The Blériot did that."

"No, you're good."

"You don't mind?"

"Mind what? That you're a girl flyer?"

"Most men don't feel so sure about that. Especially since my machine is better than theirs."

"Well, I wouldn't feel so sure about racing you!"

She laughed. "You're different, aren't you? The others are more like businessmen who decided to be flyers. I think you *had* to become a flyer. Like I did. Nothing else would be as—" She stopped, then said, "Have you ever heard that a flyer can't possibly explain what flying means, even to another flyer? It's true, isn't it?" There was a sudden mistiness in her brown-gold eyes.

"Yes," he agreed gently. "That's why we talk about engines and rigging and control wires. But all the time, we're really saying something more."

She put her empty bottle in the wooden case beside the refreshment stand. "Come on, I'll show you the Blériot."

It appeared even smaller on the ground, a little dragonfly that made his Wright seem like a flying truck. The stubby wing was braced with only a few wires stretched from single V-shaped struts extending above and below the fuselage. "The engine isn't the original Anzani," she said. "It's a seventy-horse Gnome radial. I had it put in after the Gordon Bennett race last year. The Anzani wouldn't run more than thirty minutes without doing something scary, so I took the thing to the Moisant school on Long Island and they replaced— What's so funny?"

"Flyers can't describe flying so we talk about engines."

"Anyway," she said, laughing, "the new engine made

this a very fast aeroplane. Nearly eighty miles an hour if I push it."

He inspected the Blériot from every angle, crawling beneath the wings to examine the complicated landing-gear suspension and finally, on Bunny's invitation, climbing into the narrow forward cockpit. She was right. His old Model B was crude compared to this sleek French machine.

Together they went to the meeting of flyers at McElroy's tent in the early afternoon. "You all know by now that Beachey isn't going to show," the promoter reported grimly. "Without him, the good people of Hammond aren't too excited about spending money just to watch Bunny's Blériot fly rings around your crackerboxes. I'm sorry about the way things have shaped up. Anybody got any ideas?"

"I don't see any big problem," Ben said in the silence. "Get the people out here and think of some ways to keep them amused."

"That *is* the big problem," McElroy countered. "I've got posters all over town, but take a look at that parking lot. It's as empty as the Sahara."

"But your posters have Beachey all over them," a lean horse-faced flyer said, "and word's out that Beachey ain't here."

"Let's get every machine in the air," Ben said with sudden inspiration. "Fly them all across Hammond together. That ought to prove there's something out here to see."

"Hey!" the flyer named Simmons said, his strawlike moustache bristling in excitement, "that's a hell of an idea, Mac!"

Fifteen minutes later, the field was hazy with acrid blue exhaust smoke and reeked of burning castor oil. One by one, the cumbersome Wrights, Curtisses, and Baldwins jounced into the cool afternoon. Bunny's Blériot took off last, leaping up like an eager sparrow to pass them all in five minutes and lead the long line of aeroplanes over the city.

People dashed out of stores, offices and the white frame houses of Hammond to stand gape-jawed in the street, heedless of shying horses and the jerking halts of angry autoists. Ben waved until his arm ached, wagged his wings, dipped and zoomed. The sky was alive with the stutter of engines and the flash of sunlight on varnished wood. Among them darted the Blériot, its throaty song deep under the Wright's higher pitch. Ben was in the company of flyers. There was no feeling like this anywhere else in the world.

He passed above a milling crowd in the center of town and waved them toward the air meet. They waved back and he loved them all, loved every drab earthbound soul who couldn't have the remotest inkling of the miracle up here five hundred feet over his or her head, free of earth, aloft on the softest of breezes. He urged them south with gestures and saw the Curtiss flyer off to his left make the same arm swing to the streets below.

And in minutes there was a new bustle in Hammond, then a beetlelike drift of autos worked toward the south road and became a stream of the curious who could no longer resist.

The aeroplanes landed one after another, two of them spitting water from radiator pinholes, a Baldwin yawing wildly before it touched down, its broken rudder-control wire whipcracking in the slipstream.

"You got us the crowd, all right." McElroy grinned at the pilots clustered around the headquarters tent. "Now I'd better change things around some, to keep them occupied. We'll give them a race to that farm over there. That's about three miles, I'd say. Three laps around would make it eighteen miles. We'll have the altitude contest. And Bunny can demonstrate speed flying. But we're still in trouble without Beachey. I wish—"

"Schedule me in his spot," Ben said. It was as if fate had sprung a big joke on him. Once a showman, always a showman. He'd forced Fos and Murf into stunt flying, and now he couldn't get out of it himself.

McElroy eyed him, stroking his thin little moustache with a forefinger. "Why should I schedule you?"

"Because I'm different from these other flyers. I haven't been trying to set speed or height records. I'm a carnival flyer. That's what you need here. Tell your announcer to play up . . ." He paused. He hadn't liked Rathrock's nickname for him, but it had grabbed the imagination of the carnival crowds. "Tell him to play up 'Suicide Horner' as your final event. Tell him I'm going to do Hoxsey's 'Dive of Death.' "

McElroy hadn't failed completely as a promoter. He had extracted five hundred dollars from the Chamber of Commerce for the speed purse and another five hundred from the Merchant's Association for the altitude contest. Bunny took the speed award handily, leading in every lap against a string of flyers who were all secretly hoping the Blériot would throw a piston rod or spring an oil leak. "Nothing fatal, you understand," one of the nonparticipating Baldwin flyers told Ben as they watched the monoplane blare past a straining Curtiss. "Just enough to put her down for a while."

A rattling Wright surprised everyone by climbing to nearly ten thousand feet before the gray-suited airman spiraled hastily back to earth to turn in his official recording barometer. There was some suspense in that flight. Arch Hoxsey had dived to his death on an altitude attempt in 1910, and the announcer made sure everyone knew it.

At five o'clock, he boomed into his "Suicide Horner" spiel. He was good enough at it to make Ben feel the same icy chill that must have been rippling through the spectators. He was going to try something he'd never done before.

Was it the size of the crowd that inspired him, or was it the fact that he was entirely on his own for the first time? He was about to break rules that Fos had drilled into him—years ago, it seemed. *Don't ever strap yourself in. The engine'll flatten you in a crash.* But Ben had gotten a stout leather belt from one of the other flyers, had chiseled slots in the Wright's plywood seat, and threaded the belt in place.

Don't let the size of the crowd get you into something new 'thout trying it first on your own. Fos had said that, too. But Ben was going to do this stunt for the first time today, in front of the largest crowd he'd ever seen.

He stepped from one of the hangar tents in his snow-white coveralls. The other pilots wore the standard flyer's garb of the day: assorted business suits and caps. Only Bunny showed any flair with her riding breeches. Now his whites caught every eye. He strode along the front of the roped-off crowd to his tattered Wright, feeling the effect of their awe but trying not to show it.

Suddenly a burst of confidence washed through him. He could do anything! He was going to fly the Dive of Death the way it should be flown, not the shallow imitation way he and Fos had flown it for Rathrock's rubes, but the vertical plunge even McElroy's gentlemen flyers would never forget. He was going to fly the Dive of Death the way Hoxsey had flown it while he lived.

161

He buckled himself into the seat. Simmons swung one of the dual propellers. The old engine clattered into life. Suddenly the wonderful perfume of newly cut grass was stronger than Ben had ever remembered. He could smell the earth itself. And the tang of gasoline, which he hardly ever noticed, was alive in his nostrils, undercut with the rich aroma of varnish and hot oil. A stab of apprehension shot through him. Was this how a flyer felt when he knew he could die? He shook himself free of the thought with an angry shove of the throttle.

The Blériot, returning from fast runs across the crowd, landed a hundred yards away as he taxied to the downwind end of the field near the road, now cluttered with automobiles. He kicked the Wright around with a hard blast of the propellers against the canted rudder, waited for the Blériot to clear, then opened the throttle. He saw Bunny wave as he sped past, but he dared not let go of either control lever. The Wright bounced free. He climbed steeply, then changed his mind and dropped toward the crowd surging against the ropes beyond the hangar line.

He wanted to thrill them, but at the same time he felt an anger that he had to work off first. He didn't hate them because they came in secret hope of seeing a flyer smash into the earth. They couldn't help that any more than he could help his urge to play on it. He and Mac had settled on a one-hundred-dollar fee for what he was about to do, but he would have done it anyway. He resented the crowd's need to turn the air meet into a circus, and he resented his own eagerness to be a part of that.

He pitched the aeroplane down, knifing through the air toward the spectators. The Wright swooped to the grass tips, then rose steeply over them, spraying oil and hot-water droplets and churning up a swirl of dust and paper scraps. Ben looked back through the tail booms. Let them chew on that for a while! He set the machine in a circling climb and felt the new security of the belt across his lap.

The sky was rimmed above the south horizon with a fluff of tiny clouds. A gentle current rocked his wings, then he climbed into glassy-smooth air. The Wright seemed to hang motionless, its engine sending tremors through the frame. He drifted upward in a peaceful sea, loving its coolness and its crystal sting on his cheeks. The earth tilted gently as he rose, turned slowly beneath him. The earth moved, but he was motionless in space.

Nearly half a mile higher than he had ever flown before, he leveled the machine. His hands tightened with the realization of what he was about to do just to amuse people to whom he owed nothing at all. Flyers *were* different. Why else would Hoxsey, Ely, Moisant, Kelly—any of them—have fatally trusted in machines of spruce, bamboo, and wire to prove they belonged in the sky?

He cut power quickly and shoved the elevator control hard. The sudden move hung him against the seat belt, the aeroplane falling out from under him. The horizon leaped above his head. He stared straight down into the distant clustered autos, tents, and aeroplanes of the air meet.

The idling propellers began to windmill against the rush of air. He heard their long drive chains whir faster around their sprockets. The whine of wind in the wires shrilled higher and drowned out all other sound. Then the wires' wail shrieked in his ears, a sound he would never hear again without his stomach clutching up under his ribs, his heart thudding in his ears, his palms wet.

The field raced upward and details popped out at him: the many colors of the crowd, the birdlike look of the parked aeroplanes, the patterns of the tent tops. He was fascinated, firmly in the seat now, wind hammering his chest, tearing at his goggles. The ground grew magically larger.

It was too close! He pulled hard on the elevator control, and it fought him like a solid fence post. Then the vertical plunge broke. Blood drained from his face and he struggled against the sudden heaviness in his legs and arms. The Wright shuddered, and above his head something cracked with the sharp punch of a pistol shot.

Was that explosive crack what Hoxsey had heard when his Wright began to disintegrate five hundred feet over Los Angeles? Ben forced himself to concentrate on the machine. It was trying to break up! Continuing the hard pullout would collapse the old kite. He eased the elevator control forward and let the Wright nose down again.

The wind shrieked louder through the bracing wires, but he felt the strain of the pullout lessen. This time, he nursed the machine out of its dive a degree at a time as the ground raced toward him.

He couldn't make it! The balance between a strain that

would split the wings and an arc that would just miss the ground was too delicate. He had to risk tightening the pullout.

The Wright rose against the hard pull of centrifugal force and gravity. His cheeks sagged. Above his head, breaking wood crackled again. The aeroplane raced across the field. Its wheels struck the roadway at the far end. Ben's head was thrown forward. Then the machine was back in the air.

He fed in power and worked the battered Wright slowly around the perimeter of the parking area. He dared not climb higher. There was a frightening mushiness in the wing warping control. He slewed his turns around with the rudder lever.

The biplane limped to the east end of the field. He was making a downwind approach, but he had to go through with it. The machine creaked and popped over the engine's racket. He could feel its structural weakness in the sloppy way it handled.

The field swung ahead of him. He cut the power as much as he dared and dragged in, tail low, hanging on the drumming propellers. The wheels found grass, began their bumping. The aeroplane settled in hard, and he knew the old Model B had begun to die.

Bunny ran from the tie-down line, trailed by a swarm of other flyers, mechanics, and spectators who had ducked under the ropes. Ben switched off the ignition. The engine choked off with a tremor that shook the whole frame.

He unbuckled his belt with numb fingers and looked down into Bunny's round little face. In that moment, he knew why he'd done the Dive of Death. Not because of the crowd; not for McElroy's hundred dollars. He had done it because of her.

She decided that he was unhurt, and she ducked under

the wings, trotted backward past the tail, and stood on tiptoe. "Fabric on the wing is all rumpled," she called.

He slid from his wing perch and stumbled toward her on rubber legs.

"It sounded like a cannon down here," she said.

A dark little mechanic Ben had seen at a Curtiss tent peered at the undersurface of the top wing and twanged the flying wires. "Main spar. I can see the break. Messy one."

Ben could never replace a wing spar—not even if Murf were here to help. "It's finished," he said. His voice faltered and he couldn't risk more words.

Bunny looked at him, then quickly looked away. The crowd pressed around to jabber and stare.

Ben's face froze in shock. When he'd taken off, he'd had everything. Then, in an instant, he had nothing, not even an old drunken straight-and-level flyer named Fos to fall back on. Nothing and nobody.

"They'll push it to the line and tie it down for you," Bunny said gently. "Come into Hammond with us."

He hunched over the big round table in the corner of the hotel taproom. Across from him, pixie-faced Simmons twitched his moustache, and around the table were the horse-faced Baldwin operator named Harve, a half dozen Curtiss and Wright flyers whose names he couldn't remember, and Bunny Daye. The management had made some noise about bringing a girl in here, even one in riding breeches and a jacket, but the flyers had made even more noise and had swept her right past the headwaiter.

A grin split Simmons' sun-cooked face, and he slid a foamy pitcher across the varnished tabletop. "For Pete's sake, Horner, this is supposed to be something like a celebration. Get started on some beer."

"I'm in mourning for a dead aeroplane."

"You'd better drink to a live flyer. When that thing let go, we figured you was Hoxsey all over again," Simmons said, jiggling the country-boy lock over his creased forehead. "You're still in one hunk. Drink to that."

Glasses went up around the table. Ben welcomed the beer's bitter coldness after the hours on the hot air-meet field. "Where's our grub?" a Curtiss man shouted.

Steaming platters of spareribs, boiled potatoes, green beans, and cole slaw arrived. "And bring us a bottle of brandy!" the noisy Curtiss flyer called after the retreating waiter. "Gotta liven up this shindig."

The brandy made the beer taste odd, but all of them were splashing it in their glasses, and Ben was carried along. A Wright flyer, who Ben learned was called "Patchy," with no apparent last name—or was that his last name?—called the strange-tasting drink a "broken spar" in honor of Ben's stunt that afternoon. After two of them, he spent half the time on his feet waving his cigar around and yelling for more of everything.

Simmons' grin kept rippling across his face and finally stayed there permanently. Two of the flyers began talking to no one at all, both at once, neither making any sense.

"What's the good of a speed race?" somebody shouted. "Nobody can beat Bunny. Some joke!"

"Nobody can beat her aeroplane," Ben heard somebody yell back. "It's not her, it's her aeroplane." They all looked at him, and he realized the loud mouth had been his own. So what? It was true. "It's her aeroplane," he repeated. "If I had one like it, I could beat anybody."

Across the table, Simmons said through his frozen grin, "So get one. We all would if we had the dough and could find one."

"It's the affordin' it," Harve Horseface said. "I know where there is a Blériot. Think it's a Blériot. Fella tried to sell it to me in December. Or was it January? Could have been January. There was snow on the ground. . . ."

"Where was it?" Ben asked.

"Before Christmas. That's where."

"Come on, Harve," Ben insisted. "*Where* was it?"

"Up in . . . Where the devil was it? Up in Milwaukee? Yeah, near some town called . . . What was it, Patchy? You was with me."

"Glendale or something. Yeah, Glendale. North of Wilmauk . . . Milwaukee. Guy named Toban. Wanted a thousand bucks for it."

"Think he still has it?" Ben pressed.

Who's got a thousand bucks?" . . .

"I'm going to call him." Ben shoved his chair back.

"*You* got a thousand bucks?" Patchy's black caterpillar eyebrows sailed upward in his square face.

"No." Ben sat down again, glad enough to do it because something had happened to the floor. It had tilted.

"Even if your machine was in one piece," Simmons said, "you've done the big stunt already. Only thing they'll pay to see now would be an actual crash."

"They nearly got that today for a bonus." Ben made wet rings on the tabletop with his glass. The Wright wasn't good for anything now. He might as well have crashed her and given them their money's— "Hey! Think about this for a minute! Suppose McElroy was to announce all over— Where the heck are we?" His brain was working sideways.

"Hammond," someone offered.

"Announce all over Hammond that somebody was going to smash his aeroplane *on purpose!*" He looked around the table in the sudden silence. "Well?"

"Be a whale of an attraction," Simmons said, more soberly than his grin indicated. "But you'd need a maniac to do it."

Ben stood up in a rush, then grabbed the table edge to keep from sliding down the slanted floor. "Get me McElroy," he cried. "Tell him I'm his maniac!"

"What a stunt!" Patchy yelled, the cigar bobbing in the corner of his mouth. "I think Mac's in the lobby." He scurried off before Simmons could stop him.

"You're not in too good a shape for decisions, Horner, you know that?" Simmons said. "You don't even know what you're saying."

"I certainly do," Ben insisted. "I'll crash the Wright for what it takes to get that Blériot in . . . Where was it?"

"Wishconsin," Harve Horseface offered.

"See, you're in worse shape than I am."

"No, I'm not. You're just wishin'."

"Patchy says you want to crash your machine on purpose," McElroy said, suddenly appearing over Ben's shoulder. "How much you want?"

"This has gone far enough," Bunny said. "Ben, let me get you out of here before you're in trouble. You don't know what you're doing."

"I know what I'm doing, all right." Ben shook off her hand. "I want a thousand dollars, McEllery."

"Son of a gun is serious," Simmons decided. "At least let's find out if there really is a Blériot in Glendale. I'll make a call."

Bunny covered Ben's glass, and Harve poured two ounces of beer over her hand before he could stop himself. Simmons was gone a full fifteen minutes while Ben watched the room gently sway in the cigar smoke. Then Simmons was back, his yellow hair dangling in Ben's face. "Hey! They were right! Guy's got a Blériot Eleven with a Gnome on it. Like Bunny's. How about that?"

If he'd had any doubts, they were gone now. "How

170

much?" Ben asked, working hard to keep his words straight.

"I bargained a little for you. Eight hundred fifty. But in cash. No trades."

"I won't have anything to trade."

"I can swing five hundred," McElroy said.

"Booo, McElroy!" Harve Horseface had come back to life. "Booo!"

"Hey, hold it down, will you?" McElroy pleaded.

"Booo! Cheap, cheap!"

"Six hundred?"

"I'll take . . ." Ben began, but Bunny put her tough little fingers over his mouth.

"Let them do it," she said close to his ear. "They all know each other. It's a game. Harve likes you."

"Why should he?"

"Nobody ever knows why Harve's like he is."

"Eight hundred," Harve said, his long face unruffled.

"Ahhh," McElroy moaned. "You sure you're going to go through with this?" he asked Ben. "Ahhh, seven . . ."

"Booo!"

". . . fifty."

"You got the other hundred from that Dive of Death today," Harve told Ben. " 'Raay, McElroy! Good ol' Mac! He gonna let the kid kill hisself for seven hundred fifty bucks!"

There was a silence, then McElroy shocked everybody. "Drinks all around!" he roared. "On me!"

"You've had enough," Bunny said to Ben. He glared at her. She met his eyes, then stared down at her fingernails. "Your funeral," she said softly.

"No way to put it," he said with great effort, and that was his last memory of the evening.

171

He awoke with blinding light pounding into his eyeballs. It was the sun beneath the half-open shade. He rolled away from it with a groan. After a totally confused moment, he decided he was in a hotel room with someone snoring in the other bed. When the someone grunted and flopped over, it turned out to be Simmons.

Ben's head thudded like the old Wright engine horribly out of tune. He swung his stockinged feet to the floor and sat on the edge of the bed with his head in his hands.

"You went down like a partridge full of birdshot," Simmons said. "Me and Harve and Bunny got you up here."

"She saw me . . . undressed like this?"

"Woman does a man's job, she gets to see what a man sees. What do you care?" He fumbled for his watch on the small table between the beds. "Gawd! It's near ten o'clock! By now, I'd say Mac's made you the best-known idiot in town."

Simmons was right. While he and Ben had a quick cup of coffee in the empty hotel dining room, an unusual number of people seemed to find reasons to pass the big arched doorway to the lobby and pause to peer at their table.

"That's him! That's him!" Ben heard one of them say. "That's the fella gonna crash his airyplane on purpose!" The others stared.

"Just between us," Ben confided to Simmons on the way to the flying field in a rattling two-cylinder Maxwell driven by one of the Wright mechanics, "I woke up this morning hoping it all was a bad dream."

"Oh, it's real enough," the straw-haired flyer said, a little too agreeably. "What I don't understand is how you let yourself get into it. You done anything like this before?"

"If you mean, have I done something as stupid, I have.

Know how I got the money for the Wright in the first place? Got shot out of a cannon. Not just once. Three times."

Simmons squinted at him, something close to admiration on his face. "I'm not so sure we need Beachey, after all."

They fought through a traffic jam as they bounced closer to the field. The place was swarming with people. "Out to see a Sunday massacree," their sun-baked driver said. "Ol' Mac's making a pile today!"

The event was set for five o'clock, allowing plenty of time for the crowd to build. "It's going to be the biggest thing that ever hit this part of the country," McElroy announced happily to Ben. "I've even sent telegrams to some friends of mine up in Chicago. They've got the word around there, too. Folks just got time to get here by train. Don't think I've ever heard of anybody smashing up an aeroplane on purpose before. It's some draw, believe you me!"

Bunny drummed her Blériot back and forth, keeping the crowd on its toes until the precision flying and spot-landing events got underway. Tame stuff. The crowd would have their tongues hanging out by the time five o'clock came.

Ben retreated to the shade of a Curtiss tent and concentrated on just how he was going to live up to what his big mouth had gotten him into. Bunny landed prettily, and a few minutes later she found him and sat in the grass next to him with her stubby little legs crossed.

"Air's nice today. Cool, smooth."

"Why don't you just come out and say it's no day to kill myself?"

"Well, is it?" Her voice was casual, but those ginger eyes held his.

"I'm noted for doing idiotic things to promote aviation." He pulled a grass blade from between his teeth and tossed it away with a sideways swing. "I want that Blériot, Bunny. More than anything I've ever wanted. More than I wanted the Wright, and I did something dumb to get that, too."

She was silent for a long thoughtful moment. "If you're determined to do it, then," she said, "have you figured out exactly how?"

"I've been working on it." He glanced at her. She wore a little frown of concentration. "Suppose I plant two posts in the ground, about twenty feet apart—"

"And fly right between them!" she said. "That would smash up the aeroplane, but what would . . . A haystack! You could have a big pile of hay just past the posts. When the Wright stopped, you'd be thrown forward."

"Right into the skid bracing wires. I'll take them off. It ought to hold together long enough to get around the field once. That's it! Let's find McElroy."

By four thirty, two six-inch hardwood posts nine feet long had been planted a full yard deep in the turf in front of the massive crowd that now bulged along both the north and south sides of the flying field. The hay had been forked out of a wagon from a nearby farm. With a borrowed mechanic, Ben bolted three-foot wooden splints along the top and bottom of the split wing spar.

The crowd was in a noisy lather of excitement by four forty-five. By five, they were close to uncontrollable. If Ben had any last-minute doubts, they were lost in the roar from thousands of throats as he finally trotted out to the old machine a few minutes past five. The engine fired up almost eagerly for the ancient Wright's suicide. He took a long last look at Bunny, eyed the gaping crowd with distaste, and fed in the gas.

With the wire bracing removed between the landing skids forward of the wings, the weakened airframe barely held together. Safety belt unbuckled, he nursed the

174

tattered biplane off the turf and cleared the roadway across the west end of the field.

The air, smooth as a lake, rushed cool against him. Bunny had watched him climb into the high perch on the lower wing, part of her seeming to protest the whole insane idea. But at the same time, another part of her estimated his chances, her eyes darting professionally over the hastily repaired upper wing, then moving on to the two posts and the pile of hay in midfield.

He eased into a shallow turn and held his breath. The controls were sluggish in their response. The field, a green island in a sea of spectators and endless acres of black automobiles, drifted beneath his wings. He leveled out and limped eastward toward the final turn.

The final turn. The old machine's last turn. He was glad Fos and Murf weren't here to see this, not after all the days and nights they'd given the battered Wright just to keep it alive. This was the same aeroplane he'd ridden that glorious afternoon at the Clarkston picnic grounds so unbelievably long ago. This was the same machine that had taught him to fly.

The field fell behind. He moved the rudder and wing warping levers. The Wright creaked around. The field rolled out ahead of him. He bumped through a nasty patch of rough air, rising, then dropping abruptly. The top wing popped above the stutter of the engine. The machine sagged. Ben leaned forward, urging the old Wright on.

He was afraid to move anything, so delicate had become the balance of forces acting on the machine. The distant posts stuck up like raw matchsticks, framing the little mound of hay he was supposed to hit. The stunt was ridiculous! His hands were shaking on the controls. How had he let himself get into this idiocy!

A rock-strewn pasture unrolled beneath him, then the

hedgerow marking the field boundary whisked past. He was sinking too fast. He palmed the throttle forward.

The crowd pressed in from both sides of the landing space, narrowing the open grass to less than a hundred feet. The engine skipped, and he heard the wires' wail. Then the big cylinders hammered again, full open, and shook the aeroplane from front to tail.

The vibration turned his cheeks to jelly, blurred his view of the oncoming posts. The Wright was dying. Too high. He stuck her down, dived off twenty feet and flared out with the wheels ticking grass.

The posts first drifted lazily toward him, then rushed forward, two stiff arms reaching to batter him out of the air. A gust lifted the right wings. The dual left wheels struck the ground, rebounded, threw the right wheels down. He fought for control, but it was too late for that. Before he was ready, the posts thudded into the wings.

The control levers were wrenched from his hands. He flailed through the air, with the sky and ground spinning around him, and plunged into the hay barrier. His breath blasted out of his lungs and the ground slammed his shoulders through the hay cushion. Then he lay in softness, stunned, not able even to shove away the hay that had closed over him to block out the sky.

A distant *woof!* came through the stillness. He heard shouts. A crackling rose around him. He choked on bitter smoke, forced his legs beneath him, and burst out of the burning mound. Almost on top of him, the Wright seethed bright flame. Its fabric seared off in yellow bursts. The oil and gasoline flared red, smoke already mounting high and black in the afternoon sky.

"But there was only a gallon of gas in it!" he protested to no one in particular. The cheering crowd pressed in. Suddenly Bunny burst through them to throw her arms around him, laughing and crying at the same time. Then she led him through the goggle-eyed people, who closed in to snatch up whatever souvenirs weren't too hot to grab.

"You're an impossible madman!" she said as they pushed through the crowd. She thrust an envelope into his hands. "Here. Mac said I could give it to you." Her voice was odd, and she turned away from his glance.

At the tie-down line, they found breathing space. He took her by the shoulders. "For a flyer, you worry a lot," he told her. "That stunt's no worse than being shot out of a cannon." He moved the edge of his thumb gently below her eye. "That must be from the smoke," he said, laughing because he had replaced the tear with an oily smudge.

Over her shoulder, he saw the Wright's naked wing frames crumple. Now the wreckage was no more than ashes and a tangle of blackened wires across the still-burning engine.

"I wish it hadn't burned. I could have sold the parts." He didn't mean that. The old machine had died in a fair imitation of glory, the way it should have.

"I need a lift into town," he said to the other flyers who had crowded around him. "Anybody know when the next train leaves for Milwaukee?"

"I'll drive you into Hammond personal," Harve Horse-face shouted. "Hey, Porky, lemme borrow your Oakland, give a flyer a hand."

Ben started through the backslapping crowd after Harve, then caught himself and grabbed Bunny's arm. "Will you wait for me?"

"Depends," she said. "I don't know what McElroy's got planned. Depends."

The sign caught his eye in the Chicago railroad station.

AUTO RACING!

AURORA SPEEDWAY

Today—2 P.M.

Wishart! Mulford!
Rickenbacher!
Pepperidge!
. . . and more!!!

Pepperidge! The Blériot in Milwaukee could wait a few hours. He ran to catch a westbound train and was in the ragged outskirts of Aurora by early afternoon. The auto-racing setup was new to him: a huge oval of wooden planks tightly banked at the ends, with towering open bleachers along the straightaways. But the crowd was the same, no mistaking that. Their eyes glittered with the blood wish, and the talk was of past disasters. "Seen Art Griener's mechanic get it at Indianapolis last year," a derby-hatted salesman type burst out to Ben. "Ever see anything like that?"

"I'm not much of an auto-race follower."

The man grunted. "Ought to be some excitement today. Track's getting wore. Them boards are likely to throw splinters when they get that way."

Ben didn't answer, and the man turned back to his study of the brightly painted Marmons, Loziers, a dashing blue Duesenberg, and a wheezing yellow Locomobile, number 34. Ben recognized the gray cockscomb as the driver pulled on his leather helmet. Fos!

"You know him? The driver in thirty-four?" Ben asked the salesman.

"Pepperidge? Real down-and-outer. Don't win much. Always tries hard, don't win often. They only put his name on the posters 'cause he usta be a pretty big name."

On this small closed track, there was no need to carry a mechanic, and the cars' second seats were empty. Snorting and blasting blue exhaust, the dozen racers rolled smoothly around the boards, then the white starting cable was lowered across the raceway. The autos lined up in a growing cloud of smoke.

Ben made out Fos's face, deeply shadowed by the bright sun, small and drawn behind the big goggles. A twist of apprehension clutched Ben's stomach.

The starting cable whipped upward. The dozen engines howled. The racers leaped forward, tires scrabbling on the boards. Before half a lap was completed, a green Marmon belched a gob of black smoke and stuttered into the infield.

The autos blared past the stands with a deafening howl. The salesman leaped up, his derby in his hand, and shouted in wild excitement, waving the drivers on. Behind the racing cars, a wash of splinters settled on the track.

A heavy Olds took the lead, but it spun out on the far turn and was narrowly avoided as the other autos skittered past. In the confusion, Fos deftly slipped into third place. Maybe the old flyer had been right, Ben thought. Maybe he was more at home here than in the sky. The race became a teeth-gritting duel to hold position on the inside of the tight turns.

Five laps. Fos still clung to his third-place position. Ben's eyes searched the infield, moved rapidly over the ragtag pits with their grease-smeared mechanics. There he was—Murf, old Murf leaning on a stack of gas tins, chewing that big cud of tobacco as if he didn't have a worry in the world. But Ben knew what he must be thinking.

On the sixteenth lap, the salesman nudged Ben hard. "Lookee there! Lookee there! What did I tell you? That track's coming apart just like I knew it would. Ohee, now for the fun!"

A Lozier caught the break first, the driver jouncing hard in the open seat, then wrenching the big steering wheel in a fight for control. The autos behind him split left and right to miss the rapidly growing hole in the wooden raceway.

Fos had shot into second place when the Duesenberg's driver misjudged his recovery from the track's steep banking. The drivers were tiring, and their handling was becoming sloppy.

Now the lead auto, a scarlet Marmon, roared down the

stretch with Fos hot on his tail. The goggled driver swung around for a quick look, and in that instant, his front right wheel caught the hole in the track. A chunk of planking as long as a man's arm flew into the air. The Marmon fishtailed, then careened into the next turn.

The broken planking fell in a long curve. Fos saw it coming. He tried to swerve, but he wasn't fast enough. The chunk of wood caught him on the side of the head. He sagged backward over the gasoline tank behind the seats. His Locomobile roared straight ahead, bounded across the sloped turn entry, and flew over the edge of the track.

Women's screams pierced the crowd's eerie groan, but the salesman beside Ben was jumping up and down in excitement. A jangling crash swallowed the crowd noise, and a balloon of black smoke leaped from beyond the track's rim.

The crowd scrambled along the bleacher seats to get a better look, shoved past Ben, pushed him down on the hard bench. He stayed there long after the gawkers had jammed against each other at the end of the grandstand to gape down at the flaming wreckage. Then he walked slowly out of the speedway to the streetcar line.

"He ain't dead," a girl's voice said behind him. "They say he's bunged up real bad, but he ain't dead, Harry."

Ben swung around. The girl was white-faced under her broad-brimmed yellow hat. "You sure of that?" he asked her.

"Sure she's sure," said the slim boy who had taken her arm to help her aboard the trolley. "We heard they're taking him to the hospital in Aurora in an undertaker's wagon. Look! There they go now!"

Ben was irresistibly drawn to the hospital, hating its smell of disinfectant, its starched rustle of impending

181

death. But he couldn't leave without going there. Murf leaned against the wall at the far end of the second-floor corridor, still wearing his stained coveralls. He stared through the narrow window at the fine rain that had begun to fall at sundown. Fos's shabby suitcase was on a nearby bench.

"Murf?"

The shambling mechanic didn't turn. "Yeah?"

"Murf, how is he?"

"Bad. He's real bad . . . *Bells afire!*" He whirled. "Ben, is that really you?"

"I saw the race. Saw it happen."

"He's gonna be near blind, Ben. If he lives at all. He ain't come out of it yet. Leg's busted. An arm shot, too. I don't care, long's he pulls through. I love that little fella. We seen each other through a lot."

He turned back to the window for a long moment, his shoulders shaking. Then he got control of himself again. "What brings you up to this neck of the woods, Ben? What you been doing with yourself these days?"

"Still flying. Doing air shows now. Me and Beachey, two of a kind." He couldn't bring himself to tell Murf about the old Wright. "Look, are you going to be able to get Fos what he needs?"

"Aw, don't worry 'bout us, Ben. We're all set. We been doing fine. Won a couple big ones. Really set us up."

Ben nodded, but he remembered what the salesman had told him about Fos at the auto track.

The door to the room nearest them opened, and a doctor in wrinkled whites motioned. "Stay here a minute, will you, Ben?" Murf asked. He walked into the room like a man carrying a ton on his back, and the door shut behind him.

Ben sat on the bench fingering the suitcase. What did it

all mean . . . the struggle to be something bigger than you were, the little tricks you used, the people you walked on . . . What did all that mean in the end?

He fiddled with the suitcase handle, then he made the decision. He knew Murf would never go along with it face-to-face, but he could do it this way. He unsnapped the catches.

Murf reappeared a few minutes later, his face gray. "No change, Ben." He made a hard effort to smile. "Mebbe after the surgery and with some luck and hope, old Fos'll have a chance. Gonna cost plenty, but we'll make out somehow. You're sure welcome to stay, Ben, but there ain't a thing you can do.

The predawn train ride back to Chicago, then south, seemed to last forever, and when the train pulled into Hammond, Ben wasn't sure why he'd come back.

"McElroy's bunch? They pulled out early this morning," the hotel clerk told him. "Don't know where they're going from here."

"Can you find somebody to take me out to the fairgrounds?"

"For what? They're gone, son." The desk clerk studied Ben's face. "Okay, okay, if that's what you want. Friend of mine'll take you out there for a couple bucks."

The air meet had evaporated, but a single aeroplane remained, shimmering white in the midday heat. She stood with one hand resting on the wing while he climbed out of the Ford and paid off the driver. The lizzie clattered away, leaving a thin dust cloud to settle along the empty lane.

"You came back," Bunny said softly.

He dropped his bags. "You waited."

"But where's your Blériot? Wasn't there one in Milwaukee after all?"

"I never got there. Spent the money."

"What do you mean, you spent the money? All eight hundred dollars?"

"Gambled all of it."

She stared at him. "You're crazy!" But she let it go at that. "We're both crazy, Ben." She held his eyes a few seconds, then ran her hand along the wing covering. "This is the fastest aeroplane in this part of the country. We could win any race a promoter like McElroy could dream up."

"You could. It's your aeroplane."

"I wouldn't admit it to anybody but you, but I can use help. I'm only a fair mechanic. I watched you work on that old Wright. You're good, Ben. Really good."

"A lady flyer and her mechanic?"

"Two flyers. We'll soon make enough to get you that Blériot."

He was tempted, truly tempted. "Look, Bunny, this time I want to be *really* free—free to fly how and where I want to."

Her sparkling ginger eyes were steady on his. "I'll go wherever you go, Ben."

"Two vagabond flyers?"

"Two freelance flyers."

"It's crazy!" He laughed. "We'll probably starve to death right here in the land of plenty." He began to laugh again, then suddenly he pulled her to him and kissed her hard.

"Ben, oh, Ben," she breathed, her arms tight around his neck. "You're not nearly as tough as you pretend to be."

"That's for having a lot more faith in me than I deserve," he said. "Come on, let's see if I'll fit in that back cockpit with this baggage of mine."

The Blériot rose gracefully off the field, its shadow racing across the burned splotch where the Wright had died. She controlled it without effort, a born flyer. The sky

184

was adrift with puffs of the lightest cumulus. The ground begin to unroll beneath the Blériot's big wire wheels, a carpet of greens, browns, and tans jeweled with flashes of sunlight on small lakes.

They hung in the glassy air, and she pointed southeast, where McElroy had told her he was going. Ben nodded. As the blunt nose swung toward Fort Wayne, he wondered what old Murf must have thought when he opened Fos's suitcase and found the neat stack of forty twenty-dollar bills.